The Joy of Revolution

The Joy of Revolution

Ken Knabb

THEORY AND PRACTICE

1997 Ken Knabb

2017, 2013 Theory and Practice

www.theoryandpractice.org.uk

ISBN: 978-0-9956609-1-5

Contents

Chapter 1: Some Facts of Life

> "We can comprehend this world only by contesting it as a whole. . . . The root of the prevailing *lack of imagination* cannot be grasped unless one is able to *imagine what is lacking*, that is, what is missing, hidden, forbidden, and yet possible, in modern life."
>
> —Situationist International[1]

Utopia or bust

Never in history has there been such a glaring contrast between what could be and what actually exists.

It's hardly necessary to go into all the problems in the world today — most of them are widely known, and to dwell on them usually does little more than dull us to their reality. But even if we are "stoic enough to endure the misfortunes of others," the present social deterioration ultimately impinges on us all. Those who don't face direct physical repression still have to face the mental repressions imposed by an increasingly mean, stressful, ignorant and ugly world. Those who escape economic poverty cannot escape the general impoverishment of life.

---

1 Ken Knabb (ed. and trans.), *Situationist International Anthology* (Bureau of Public Secrets, 1981), p. 81 [Revised Edition pp. 106-107]. Here and elsewhere I have sometimes slightly modified my original *SI Anthology* translations.

And even life at this pitiful level cannot continue for long. The ravaging of the planet by the global develop-ment of capitalism has brought us to the point where humanity may become extinct within a few decades.

Yet this same development has made it possible to abolish the system of hierarchy and exploitation that was previously based on material scarcity and to inaugurate a new, genuinely liberated form of society.

Plunging from one disaster to another on its way to mass insanity and ecological apocalypse, this system has developed a momentum that is out of control, even by its supposed masters. As we approach a world in which we won't be able to leave our fortified ghettoes without armed guards, or even go outdoors without applying sunscreen lest we get skin cancer, it's hard to take seriously those who advise us to beg for a few reforms.

What is needed, I believe, is a worldwide participa-tory-democracy revolution that would abolish both capitalism and the state. This is admittedly a big order, but I'm afraid that nothing less can get to the root of our problems. It may seem absurd to talk about revolution; but all the alternatives assume the continuation of the present system, which is even more absurd.

Stalinist "communism" and reformist "socialism" are merely variants of capitalism

Before going into what this revolution would involve and responding to some typical objections, it should be stressed that it has nothing to do with the repugnant stereotypes that are usually evoked by the word (terrorism, revenge, political coups, manipulative leaders preaching self-sacrifice, zombie followers chanting politically correct slogans). In particular, it should not be confused with the two principal failures of modern social change, Stalinist "communism" and reformist "socialism."

After decades in power, first in Russia and later in many other countries, it has become obvious that Stalinism is the total opposite of a liberated society. The origin of this grotesque phenomenon is less obvious. Trotskyists and others have tried to distinguish Stalinism from the earlier Bolshevism of Lenin and Trotsky. There *are* differences, but they are more of degree than of kind. Lenin's *The State and Revolution*, for example, presents a more coherent critique of the state than can be found in most anarchist writings; the problem is that the radical aspects of Lenin's thought merely ended up camouflaging the Bolsheviks' actual authoritarian practice. Placing itself above the masses it claimed to represent, and with a corresponding internal hierarchy between party militants and their leaders, the Bolshevik Party was already well on its way toward creating the conditions for the development of Stalinism while Lenin and Trotsky were still firmly in control.[2]

But we have to be clear about what failed if we are ever going to do any better. If socialism means people's full participation in the social decisions that affect their own lives, it has existed neither in the Stalinist regimes of the East nor in the welfare states of the West. The recent collapse of Stalinism is neither a vindication of capitalism nor proof of the failure of "Marxist communism." Anyone who has ever bothered to read Marx (most of his glib critics obviously have not) is aware that Leninism

---

2   See Maurice Brinton's *The Bolsheviks and Workers' Control: 1917-1921*, Voline's *The Unknown Revolution*, Ida Mett's *The Kronstadt Uprising*, Paul Avrich's *Kronstadt 1921*, Peter Arshinov's *History of the Makhnovist Movement*, and Guy Debord's *The Society of the Spectacle* §§98-113.

represents a severe distortion of Marx's thought and that Stalinism is a total parody of it. Nor does government ownership have anything to do with communism in its authentic sense of common, communal ownership; it is merely a different type of capitalism in which state-bureaucratic ownership replaces (or merges with) private-corporate ownership.

The long spectacle of opposition between these two varieties of capitalism hid their mutual reinforcement. Serious conflicts were confined to proxy battles in the Third World (Vietnam, Angola, Afghanistan, etc.). Neither side ever made any real attempt to overthrow the enemy in its own heartland. (The French Communist Party sabotaged the May 1968 revolt; the Western powers, which intervened massively in countries where they were not wanted, refused to send so much as the few antitank weapons desperately needed by the 1956 Hungarian insurgents.) Guy Debord noted in 1967 that Stalinist state-capitalism had already revealed itself as merely a "poor cousin" of classical Western capitalism, and that its decline was beginning to deprive Western rulers of the pseudo-opposition that reinforced them by seeming to represent the sole alternative to their system. "The bourgeoisie is in the process of losing the adversary that objectively supported it by providing an illusory unification of all opposition to the existing order" (*The Society of the Spectacle,* §§110-111).

Although Western leaders pretended to welcome the recent Stalinist collapse as a natural victory for their own system, none of them had seen it coming and they now obviously have no idea what to do about all the problems it poses except to cash in on the situation before it totally falls apart. The monopolistic multinational corporations that proclaim "free enterprise" as a panacea are quite aware that free-market capitalism would long ago have exploded from its own contradictions had it not been saved despite itself by a few New Deal-style pseudosocialist reforms.

Those reforms (public services, social insurance, the eight-hour day, etc.) may have ameliorated some of the more glaring defects of the system, but in no way have they led beyond it. In recent years they have not even kept up with its accelerating crises. The most significant improvements were in any case won only by long and often violent popular struggles that eventually forced the hands of the bureaucrats: the leftist parties and labor unions that pretended to lead those struggles have functioned primarily as safety valves, coopting radical tendencies and greasing the wheels of the social machine.

As the situationists have shown, the bureaucratization of radical movements, which has degraded people into followers constantly "betrayed" by their leaders, is linked to the increasing *spectacularization* of modern capitalist society, which has degraded people into spectators of a world over which they have no control — a development that has become increasingly glaring, though it is usually only superficially understood.

Taken together, all these considerations point to the conclusion that a liberated society can be created only by the active participation of the people as a whole, not by hierarchical organizations supposedly acting on their behalf. The point is not to choose more honest or "responsive" leaders, but to avoid granting independent power to any leaders whatsoever. Individuals or groups may initiate radical actions, but a substantial and rapidly expanding portion of the population must take part if a movement is to lead to a new society and not simply to a coup installing new rulers.

Representative democracy versus delegate democracy
I won't repeat all the classic socialist and anarchist critiques of capitalism and the state; they are already widely known, or at least widely accessible. But in order to cut through some of the confusions of traditional political rhetoric, it may be helpful to summarize the basic types of social organization. For the sake of clarity, I will start out by examining the "political" and "economic" aspects separately, though they are obviously interlinked. It is as futile to try to equalize people's economic conditions through a state bureaucracy as it is to try to democratize society while the power of money enables the wealthy few to control the institutions that determine people's awareness of social realities. Since the system functions as a whole it can be fundamentally changed only as a whole.

To begin with the political aspect, roughly speaking we can distinguish five degrees of "government":

1. Unrestricted freedom
2. Direct democracy
    a) consensus
    b) majority rule
3. Delegate democracy
4. Representative democracy
5. Overt minority dictatorship

The present society oscillates between (4) and (5), i.e. between overt minority rule and covert minority rule camouflaged by a façade of token democracy. A liberated society would eliminate (4) and (5) and would progressively reduce the need for (2) and (3).

I'll discuss the two types of (2) later on. But the crucial distinction is between (3) and (4).

In representative democracy people abdicate their power to elected officials. The candidates' stated policies are limited to a few vague generalities, and once they are elected there is little control over their actual decisions on hundreds of issues — apart from the feeble threat of changing one's vote, a few years later, to some equally uncontrollable rival politician. Representatives are dependent on the wealthy for bribes and campaign contributions; they are subordinate to the owners of the mass media, who decide which issues get the publicity; and they are almost as ignorant and powerless as the general public regarding many important matters that are determined by unelected bureaucrats and independent secret agencies. Overt dictators may sometimes be overthrown, but the real rulers in "democratic" regimes, the tiny minority who own or control virtually everything, are never voted in and never voted out. Most people don't even know who they are.

In delegate democracy, delegates are elected for specific purposes with very specific limitations. They may be strictly mandated (ordered to vote in a certain way on a certain issue) or the mandate may be left open (delegates being free to vote as they think best) with the people who have elected them reserving the right to confirm or reject any decision thus taken. Delegates are generally elected for very short periods and are subject to recall at any time.

In the context of radical struggles, delegate assemblies have usually been termed "councils." The council form was invented by striking workers during the 1905 Russian revolution (*soviet* is the Russian word for council). When soviets reappeared in 1917, they were successively supported, manipulated, dominated and coopted by the Bolsheviks, who soon succeeded in transforming them into parodies of themselves: rubber stamps of the "Soviet State" (the last surviving independent soviet, that of the Kronstadt sailors, was crushed in 1921). Councils have nevertheless continued to reappear spontaneously at the most radical moments in subsequent history, in Germany, Italy, Spain, Hungary and elsewhere, because they represent the obvious solution to the need for a practical form of nonhierarchical popular self-organization. And they continue to be opposed by all hierarchical organizations, because they threaten the rule of specialized elites by pointing to the possibility of a society of *generalized self-management*:not self-management of a few details of the present setup, but self-management extended to all regions of the globe and all aspects of life.

But as noted above, the question of democratic forms cannot be separated from their economic context.

Irrationalities of capitalism
Economic organization can be looked at from the angle of work:

1. Totally voluntary
2. Cooperative (collective self-management)
3. Forced and exploitive
   a) overt (slave labor)
   b) disguised (wage labor)

And from the angle of distribution:

1. True communism (totally free accessibility)
2. True socialism (collective ownership and regulation)
3. Capitalism (private and/or state ownership)

Though it's possible for goods or services produced by wage labor to be given away, or for those produced by volunteer or cooperative labor to be turned into commodities for sale, for the most part these levels of work and distribution tend to correspond with each other. The present society is predominately (3): the forced production and consumption of commodities. A liberated society would eliminate (3) and as far as possible reduce (2) in favor of (1).

Capitalism is based on commodity production (production of goods for profit) and wage labor (labor power itself bought and sold as a commodity). As Marx pointed out, there is less difference between the slave and the "free" worker than appears. Slaves, though they seem to be paid nothing, are provided with the means of their survival and reproduction, for which workers (who become temporary slaves during their hours of labor) are compelled to pay most of their wages. The fact that some jobs are less unpleasant than others, and that individual workers have the nominal right to switch jobs, start their own business, buy stocks or win a lottery, disguises the fact that the vast majority of people are collectively enslaved.

How did we get in this absurd position? If we go back far enough, we find that at some point people were forcibly dispossessed: driven off the land and otherwise deprived of the means for producing the goods necessary for life. (The famous chapters on "primitive accumulation" in *Capital* vividly describe this process in England.) As long as people accept this dispossession as legitimate, they are forced into unequal bargains with the "owners" (those who have robbed them, or who have subsequently obtained titles of "ownership" from the original robbers) in which they exchange their labor for a fraction of what it actually produces, the surplus being retained by the owners. This surplus (capital) can then be reinvested in order to generate continually greater surpluses in the same way.

As for distribution, a public water fountain is a simple example of true communism (unlimited accessibility). A public library is an example of true socialism (free but regulated accessibility).

In a rational society, accessibility would depend on abundance. During a drought, water might have to be rationed. Conversely, once libraries are put entirely online they could become totally communistic: anyone could have free instant access to any number of texts with no more need to bother with checking out and returning, security against theft, etc.

But this rational relation is impeded by the persistence of separate economic interests. To take the latter example, it will soon be technically possible to create a global "library" in which every book ever written, every film ever made and every musical performance ever recorded could be put online, potentially enabling anyone to freely tap in and obtain a copy (no more need for stores, sales, advertising, packaging, shipping, etc.). But since this would also eliminate the profits from present-day publishing, recording and film businesses, far more energy is spent concocting complicated methods to prevent or charge for copying (while others devote corresponding energy devising ways to get around such methods) than on developing a technology that could potentially benefit everyone.

One of Marx's merits was to have cut through the hollowness of political discourses based on abstract philosophical or ethical principles ("human nature" is such and such, all people have a "natural right" to this or that) by showing how social possibilities and social awareness are to a great degree limited and shaped by material conditions. Freedom in the abstract means little if almost everybody has to work all the time simply to assure their survival. It's unrealistic to expect people to be generous and cooperative when there is barely enough to go around (leaving aside the drastically different conditions under which "primitive communism" flourished). But a sufficiently large surplus opens up wider possibilities. The hope of Marx and other revolutionaries of his time was based on the fact that the technological potentials developed by the Industrial Revolution had finally provided an adequate material basis for a classless society. It was no longer a matter of declaring that things "should" be different, but of pointing out that they could be different; that class domination was not only unjust, it was now *unnecessary*.

Was it ever really necessary? Was Marx right in seeing the development of capitalism and the state as inevitable stages, or might a liberated society have been possible without this painful detour? Fortunately, we no longer have to worry about this question. Whatever possibilities there may or may not have been in the past, present material conditions are more than sufficient to sustain a global classless society.

The most serious drawback of capitalism is not its quantitative unfairness — the mere fact that wealth is unequally distributed, that workers are not paid the full "value" of their labor. The problem is that this margin of exploitation (even if relatively small) makes possible the private accumulation of capital, which eventually reorients everything to its own ends, dominating and warping all aspects of life.

The more alienation the system produces, the more social energy must be diverted just to keep it going — more advertising to sell superfluous commodities, more ideologies to keep people bamboozled, more spectacles to keep them pacified, more police and more prisons to repress crime and rebellion, more arms to compete with rival states — all of which produces more frustrations and antagonisms, which must be repressed by more spectacles, more prisons, etc. As this vicious circle continues, real human needs are fulfilled only incidentally, if at all, while virtually all labor is channeled into absurd, redundant or destructive projects that serve no purpose except to maintain the system.

If this system were abolished and modern technological potentials were appropriately transformed and redirected, the labor necessary to meet real human needs would be reduced to such a trivial level that it could easily be taken care of voluntarily and cooperatively, without requiring economic incentives or state enforcement.

It's not too hard to grasp the idea of superseding overt hierarchical power. Self-management can be seen as the fulfillment of the freedom and democracy that are the official values of Western societies. Despite people's submissive conditioning, everyone has had moments when they rejected domination and began speaking or acting for themselves.

It's much harder to grasp the idea of superseding the economic system. The domination of capital is more subtle and self-regulating. Questions of work, production, goods, services, exchange and coordination in the modern world seem so complicated that most people take for granted the necessity of money as a universal mediation, finding it difficult to imagine any change beyond apportioning money in some more equitable way.

For this reason I will postpone more extensive discussion of the economic aspects till later in this text, when it will be possible to go into more detail.

Some exemplary modern revolts

Is such a revolution likely? The odds are probably against it. The main problem is that there is not much time. In previous eras it was possible to imagine that, despite all humanity's follies and disasters, we would somehow muddle through and perhaps eventually learn from past mistakes. But now that social policies and technological developments have irrevocable global ecological ramifications, blundering trial and error is not enough. We have only a few decades to turn things around. And as time passes, the task becomes more difficult: the fact that basic social problems are scarcely even faced, much less resolved, encourages increasingly desperate and delirious tendencies toward war, fascism, ethnic antagonism, religious fanaticism and other forms of mass irrationality, deflecting those who might potentially work toward a new society into merely defensive and ultimately futile holding actions.

But most revolutions have been preceded by periods

when everyone scoffed at the idea that things could ever change. Despite the many discouraging trends in the world, there are also some encouraging signs, not least of which is the widespread disillusionment with previous false alternatives. Many popular revolts in this century have already moved spontaneously in the right direction. I am not referring to the "successful" revolutions, which are without exception frauds, but to less known, more radical efforts. Some of the most notable examples are Russia 1905, Germany 1918-19, Italy 1920, Asturias 1934, Spain 1936-37, Hungary 1956, France 1968, Czechoslovakia 1968, Portugal 1974-75 and Poland 1980-81; many other movements, from the Mexican revolution of 1910 to the recent anti-apartheid struggle in South Africa, have also contained exemplary moments of popular experimentation before they were brought under bureaucratic control.

No one is in any position to dismiss the prospect of revolution who has not carefully examined these movements. To ignore them because of their "failure" is missing the point.[3] Modern revolution is all or nothing: individual

---

3   "The journalists' and governments' superficial references to the 'success' or 'failure' of a revolution mean nothing for the simple reason that since the bourgeois revolutions *no revolution has yet succeeded:* not one has abolished classes. Proletarian revolution has so far not been victorious anywhere, but the practical process through which its project manifests itself has already created at least ten revolutionary moments of historic importance that can appropriately be termed revolutions. In none of these moments was the total content of proletarian revolution fully developed; but in each case there was a fundamental interruption of the ruling socioeconomic order and the appearance of new forms and conceptions of real life: variegated phenomena that can be understood and evaluated only in their overall significance, including their potential future significance. . . . The revolution of 1905 did not bring down the Czarist regime, it only obtained a few temporary concessions from

revolts are bound to fail until an international chain reaction is triggered that spreads faster than repression can close in. It's hardly surprising that these revolts did not go farther; what is inspiring is that they went as far as they did. A new revolutionary movement will undoubtedly take new and unpredictable forms; but these earlier efforts remain full of examples of what can be done, as well as of what must be avoided.

Some common objections

It's often said that a stateless society might work if everyone were angels, but due to the perversity of human nature some hierarchy is necessary to keep people in line. It would be truer to say that if everyone were angels the *present* system might work tolerably well (bureaucrats would function honestly, capitalists would refrain from socially harmful ventures even if they were profitable). It is precisely because people are not angels that it's necessary to eliminate the setup that enables some of them to

---

it. The Spanish revolution of 1936 did not formally suppress the existing political power: it arose, in fact, out of a proletarian uprising initiated in order to defend that Republic against Franco. And the Hungarian revolution of 1956 did not abolish Nagy's liberal-bureaucratic government. Among other regrettable limitations, the Hungarian movement had many aspects of a national uprising against foreign domination; and this national-resistance aspect also played a certain, though less important, role in the origin of the Paris Commune. The Commune supplanted Thiers's power only within the limits of Paris. And the St. Petersburg Soviet of 1905 never even took control of the capital. All the crises cited here as examples, though deficient in their practical achievements and even in their perspectives, nevertheless produced enough radical innovations and put their societies severely enough in check to be legitimately termed revolutions." (*SI Anthology*, pp. 235-236 [Revised Edition pp. 301-302]

become very efficient devils. Lock a hundred people in a small room with only one air hole and they will claw each other to death to get to it. Let them out and they may manifest a rather different nature. As one of the May 1968 graffiti put it, "Man is neither Rousseau's noble savage nor the Church's depraved sinner. He is violent when oppressed, gentle when free."

Others contend that, whatever the ultimate causes may be, people are now so screwed up that they need to be psychologically or spiritually healed before they can even conceive of creating a liberated society. In his later years Wilhelm Reich came to feel that an "emotional plague" was so firmly embedded in the population that it would take generations of healthily raised children before people would become capable of a libertarian social transformation; and that meanwhile one should avoid confronting the system head-on since this would stir up a hornet's nest of ignorant popular reaction.

Irrational popular tendencies do sometimes call for discretion. But powerful though they may be, they are not irresistible forces. They contain their own contradictions. Clinging to some absolute authority is not necessarily a sign of faith in authority; it may be a desperate attempt to overcome one's increasing doubts (the convulsive tightening of a slipping grip). People who join gangs or reactionary groups, or who get caught up in religious cults or patriotic hysteria, are also seeking a sense of liberation, connection, purpose, participation, empowerment. As Reich himself showed, fascism gives a particularly vigorous and dramatic expression to these basic aspirations, which is why it often has a deeper appeal than the vacillations, compromises and hypocrisies of liberalism and leftism.

In the long run the only way to defeat reaction is to present more forthright expressions of these aspirations, and more authentic opportunities to fulfill them. When basic issues are forced into the open, irrationalities that flourished under the cover of psychological repression tend to be weakened, like disease germs exposed to sunlight and fresh air. In any case, even if we don't prevail, there is at least some satisfaction in fighting for what we really believe, rather than being defeated in a posture of hesitancy and hypocrisy.

There are limits on how far one can liberate oneself (or raise liberated children) within a sick society. But if Reich was right to note that psychologically repressed people are less capable of envisioning social liberation, he failed to realize how much the process of social revolt can be psychologically liberating. (French psychiatrists are said to have complained about a significant drop in the number of their customers in the aftermath of May 1968!)

The notion of total democracy raises the specter of a "tyranny of the majority." Majorities *can* be ignorant and bigoted, there's no getting around it. The only real solution is to confront and attempt to overcome that ignorance and bigotry. Keeping the masses in the dark (relying on liberal judges to protect civil liberties or liberal legislators to sneak through progressive reforms) only leads to popular back-lashes when sensitive issues eventually do come to the surface.

Examined more closely, however, most instances of majority oppression of minorities turn out to be due not to majority rule, but to disguised minority rule in which the ruling elite plays on whatever racial or cultural antagonisms there may be in order to turn the exploited masses' frustrations against each other. When people get real power over their own lives they will have more interesting things to do than to persecute minorities.

So many potential abuses or disasters are evoked at any suggestion of a nonhierarchical society that it would be impossible to answer them all. People who resignedly accept a system that condemns millions of their fellow human beings to death every year in wars and famines, and millions of others to prison and torture, suddenly let their imagination and their indignation run wild at the thought that in a self-managed society there might be *some* abuses, some violence or coercion or injustice, or even merely some temporary inconvenience. They forget that it is not up to a new social system to solve all our problems; it merely has to deal with them better than the *present* system does — not a very big order.

If history followed the complacent opinions of official commentators, there would never have been any revolutions. In any given situation there are always plenty of ideologists ready to declare that no radical change is possible. If the economy is functioning well, they will claim that revolution depends on economic crises; if there is an economic crisis, others will just as confidently declare that revolution is impossible because people are too busy worrying about making ends meet. The former types, surprised by the May 1968 revolt, tried to retrospectively uncover the invisible crisis that their ideology insists must have been there. The latter contend that the situationist perspective has been refuted by the worsened economic conditions since that time.

Actually, the situationists simply noted that the wide-

spread achievement of capitalist abundance had demonstrated that guaranteed survival was no substitute for real
life. The periodic ups and downs of the economy have no
bearing on that conclusion. The fact that a few people at
the top have recently managed to siphon off a yet larger
portion of the social wealth, driving increasing numbers of
people into the streets and terrorizing the rest of the
population lest they succumb to the same fate, makes the
feasibility of a postscarcity society less evident; but the
material prerequisites are still present.

The economic crises held up as evidence that we
need to "lower our expectations" are actually caused
by *over*-production and *lack* of work. The ultimate absurdity of the present system is that unemployment is seen as
a problem, with potentially labor-saving technologies being
directed toward creating new jobs to replace the old ones
they render unnecessary. The problem is not that so many
people don't have jobs, but that so many people still do.
We need to raise our expectations, not lower them.[4]

Increasing dominance of the spectacle

Far more serious than this spectacle of our supposed
powerlessness in the face of the economy is the greatly
increased power of the spectacle itself, which in recent
years has developed to the point of repressing virtually any
awareness of pre-spectacle history or anti-spectacle possibilities. Debord's *Comments on the Society of the*

---

4   "We're not interested in hearing about the exploiters' economic
problems. If the capitalist economy is not capable of fulfilling
workers' demands, that is simply one more reason to struggle for a
new society, one in which we ourselves have the decision making
power over the whole economy and all social life." (Portuguese air-
line workers, 27 October 1974.)

Spectacle (1988) goes into this new development in detail:

> In all that has happened over the last twenty
> years, the most important change lies in the very
> continuity of the spectacle. What is significant is
> not the refinements of the spectacle's media
> instrumentation, which had already attained a
> highly advanced stage of development; it is
> quite simply that spectacular domination has
> succeeded in raising an entire generation
> molded to its laws. . . . Spectacular domination's
> first priority was to eradicate historical knowl-
> edge in general, beginning with virtually all
> information and rational commentary on the
> most recent past. . . . The spectacle makes sure
> that people are unaware of what is happening,
> or at least that they quickly forget whatever they
> may have become aware of. The more impor-
> tant something is, the more it is hidden.
> Nothing in the last twenty years has been so
> thoroughly shrouded with official lies as May
> 1968. . . . The flow of images carries everything
> before it, and it is always someone else who
> controls this simplified digest of the perceptible
> world, who decides where the flow will lead,
> who programs the rhythm of what is shown
> into an endless series of arbitrary surprises that
> leaves no time for reflection . . . . isolating what-
> ever is presented from its context, its past, its
> intentions and its consequences. . . . It is thus
> hardly surprising that children are now starting
> their education with an enthusiastic introduction
> to the Absolute Knowledge of computer

language while becoming increasingly incapable of reading. Because reading requires making judgments at every line; and since conversation is almost dead (as will soon be most of those who knew how to converse) reading is the only remaining gateway to the vast realms of pre-spectacle human experience.

In the present text I have tried to recapitulate some basic points that have been buried under this intensive spectacular repression. If these matters seem banal to some or obscure to others, they may at least serve to recall what once was possible, in those primitive times a few decades ago when people had the quaint, old-fashioned notion that they could understand and affect their own history.

While there is no question that things have changed considerably since the sixties (mostly for the worse), our situation may not be quite as hopeless as it seems to those who swallow whatever the spectacle feeds them. Sometimes it only takes a little jolt to break through the stupor.

Even if we have no guarantee of ultimate victory, such breakthroughs are already a pleasure. Is there any greater game around?

Chapter 2: Foreplay

"An individual cannot know what he really is
until he has realized himself through action. . . .
The interest the individual finds in something is
already the answer to the question of whether
he should act and what should be done."

—Hegel, *The Phenomenology of Spirit*

Personal breakthroughs

Later on I will try to answer some more of the perennial
objections. But as long as the objectors remain passive, all
the arguments in the world will never faze them, and they
will continue to sing the old refrain: "It's a nice idea, but
it's not realistic, it goes against human nature, it's always
been this way. . . ." Those who don't realize their own
potential are unlikely to recognize the potential of others.

To paraphrase that very sensible old prayer, we need
the initiative to solve the problems we can, the patience to
endure the ones we can't, and the wisdom to know the
difference. But we also need to bear in mind that some
problems that can't be solved by isolated individuals can be
solved collectively. Discovering that others share the same
problem is often the beginning of a solution.

Some problems can, of course, be solved individually,
through a variety of methods ranging from elaborate ther-

apies or spiritual practices to simple commonsense decisions to correct some mistake, break some harmful habit, try something new, etc. But my concern here is not with purely personal makeshifts, worthwhile though they may be within their limits, but with moments where people move "outward" in deliberately subversive ventures.

There are more possibilities than appear at first sight. Once you refuse to be intimidated, some of them are quite simple. You can begin anywhere. And you have to begin somewhere — do you think you can learn to swim if you never go in the water?

Sometimes a little action is needed to cut through excessive verbiage and reestablish a concrete perspective. It needn't be anything momentous; if nothing else comes to mind, some rather arbitrary venture may suffice — just enough to shake things up a bit and wake yourself up.

At other times it's necessary to stop, to break the chain of compulsive actions and reactions. To clear the air, to create a little space free from the cacophony of the spectacle. Just about everyone does this to some degree, out of instinctive psychological self-defense, whether by practicing some form of meditation, or by periodically engaging in some activity that effectively serves the same purpose (working in one's garden, taking a walk, going fishing), or simply by pausing to take a deep breath amid their daily round, coming back for a moment to the "quiet center." Without such a space it is difficult to get a sane perspective on the world, or even simply to keep one's own sanity.

One of the methods I have found most useful is to put things in writing. The advantage is partly psychological (some problems lose their power over us by being set out where we can see them more objectively), partly a matter of organizing our thoughts so as to see the different factors and choices more clearly. We often maintain inconsistent notions without becoming aware of their contradictions until we try putting them down on paper.

I have sometimes been criticized for exaggerating the importance of writing. Many matters can, of course, be dealt with more directly. But even nonverbal actions require thinking about, talking about, and usually writing about, if they are to be effectively carried out, communicated, debated, corrected.

(In any case, I don't claim to cover everything; I am merely discussing certain points about which I feel I have something to say. If you think I have failed to address some important topic, why don't you do it yourself?)

Critical interventions

Writing enables you to work out your ideas at your own pace, without worrying about oratorical skills or stage fright. You can make a point once and for all instead of having to constantly repeat yourself. If discretion is necessary, a text can be issued anonymously. People can read it at *their* own pace, stop and think about it, go back and check specific points, reproduce it, adapt it, refer others to it. Talking may generate quicker and more detailed feedback, but it can also disperse your energy, prevent you from focusing and implementing your ideas. Those in the same rut as you may resist your efforts to escape because your success would challenge their own passivity.

Sometimes you can best provoke such people by simply leaving them behind and pursuing your own course. ("Hey, wait for me!") Or by shifting the dialogue to a different level. A letter forces both writer and addressee to work out their ideas more clearly. Copies to others concerned may enliven the discussion. An open letter draws in even more people.

If you succeed in creating a chain reaction in which more and more people read your text because they see others reading it and heatedly discussing it, it will no longer be possible for anyone to pretend to be unaware of the issues you have raised.[1]

Suppose, for example, that you criticize a group for being hierarchical, for allowing a leader to have power over members (or followers or fans). A private talk with one of the members might merely meet with a series of contradictory defensive reactions with which it is fruitless to argue. ("No, he's not really our leader. . . . And even if he is, he's not authoritarian. . . . And besides, what right do you have to criticize?") But a public critique forces such contradictions into the open and puts people in a crossfire. While one member denies that the group is hierarchical, a second may admit that it is and attempt to justify this by attributing superior insight to the leader. This may cause a third member to start thinking.

At first, annoyed that you have disturbed their cozy little scene, the group is likely to close ranks around the leader and denounce you for your "negativity" or "elitist

---

1   The SI's dissemination of a text denouncing an international gathering of art critics in Belgium was a fine example of this: "Copies were mailed to a large number of critics or given to them personally. Others were telephoned and read all or part of the text. A group forced its way into the Press Club where the critics were being received and threw the leaflets among the audience. Others were tossed onto the sidewalks from upstairs windows or from a car. . . . In short, all steps were taken to leave the critics no chance of being unaware of the text." (*SI Anthology*, p. 49 [Revised Edition pp. 60-61].)

arrogance." But if your intervention has been acute enough, it may continue to sink in and have a delayed impact. The leader now has to watch his step since everyone is more sensitive to anything that might seem to confirm your critique. In order to demonstrate how unjustified you are, the members may insist on greater democratization. Even if the particular group proves impervious to change, its example may serve as an object lesson for a wider public. Outsiders who might otherwise have made similar mistakes can more easily see the pertinence of your critique because they have less emotional investment.

It's usually more effective to criticize institutions and ideologies than to attack individuals who merely happen to be caught up in them — not only because the machine is more crucial than its replaceable parts, but because this approach makes it easier for individuals to save face while dissociating themselves from the machine.

But however tactful you may be, there's no getting around the fact that virtually any significant critique will provoke irrational defensive reactions, ranging from personal attacks on you to invocations of one or another of the many fashionable ideologies that seem to demonstrate the impossibility of any rational consideration of social problems. Reason is denounced as cold and abstract by demagogues who find it easier to play on people's feelings; theory is scorned in the name of practice. . . .

Theory versus ideology
To theorize is simply to try to understand what we are doing. We are all theorists whenever we honestly discuss what has happened, distinguish between the significant and the irrelevant, see through fallacious explanations, recog-

nize what worked and what didn't, consider how something might be done better next time. Radical theorizing is simply talking or writing to more people about more general issues in more abstract (i.e. more widely applicable) terms. Even those who claim to reject theory theorize — they merely do so more unconsciously and capriciously, and thus more inaccurately.

Theory without particulars is empty, but particulars without theory are blind. Practice tests theory, but theory also inspires new practice.

Radical theory has nothing to respect and nothing to lose. It criticizes itself along with everything else. It is not a doctrine to be accepted on faith, but a tentative generalization that people must constantly test and correct for themselves, a practical simplification indispensable for dealing with the complexities of reality.

But hopefully not an oversimplification. Any theory can turn into an ideology, become rigidified into a dogma, be twisted to hierarchical ends. A sophisticated ideology may be relatively accurate in certain respects; what differentiates it from theory is that it lacks a dynamic relation to practice. Theory is when you have ideas; ideology is when ideas have you. "Seek simplicity, and distrust it."

Avoiding false choices and elucidating real ones
We have to face the fact that there are no foolproof gimmicks, that no radical tactic is invariably appropriate. Something that is collectively possible during a revolt may not be a sensible option for an isolated individual. In certain urgent situations it may be necessary to urge people to take some specific action; but in most cases it is best simply to elucidate relevant factors that people should take into account when making their own decisions. (If I occa-

sionally presume to offer direct advice here, this is for convenience of expression. "Do this" should be understood as "In some circumstances it may be a good idea to do this.")

A social analysis need not be long or detailed. Simply "dividing one into two" (pointing out contradictory tendencies within a given phenomenon or group or ideology) or "combining two into one" (revealing a commonality between two apparently distinct entities) may be useful, especially if communicated to those most directly involved. More than enough information is already available on most issues; what is needed is to cut through the glut in order to reveal the essential. Once this is done, other people, including knowledgeable insiders, will be spurred to more thorough investigations if these are necessary.

When confronted with a given topic, the first thing is to determine whether it is indeed a single topic. It's impossible to have any meaningful discussion of "Marxism" or "violence" or "technology" without distinguishing the diverse senses that are lumped under such labels.

On the other hand, it can also be useful to take some broad, abstract category and show its predominant tendencies, even though such a pure type does not actually exist. The situationists' *Student Poverty* pamphlet, for example, scathingly enumerates all sorts of stupidities and pretensions of "the student." Obviously not every student is guilty of all these faults, but the stereotype serves as a focus around which to organize a systematic critique of general tendencies. By stressing qualities most students have in common, the pamphlet also implicitly challenges those who claim to be exceptions to prove it. The same applies to the critique of "the pro-situ" in Debord and Sanguinetti's *The Real Split in the International* — a challenging rebuff of followers perhaps unique in the history of radical movements.

"Everyone is asked their opinion about every detail in order to prevent them from forming one about the totality" (Vaneigem). Many issues are such emotionally loaded tar-babies that anyone who reacts to them becomes entangled in false choices. The fact that two sides are in conflict, for example, does not mean that you must support one or the other. If you cannot do anything about a particular problem, it is best to clearly acknowledge this fact and move on to something that does present practical possibilities.[2]

---

2   "The absence of a revolutionary movement in Europe has reduced the Left to its simplest expression: a mass of spectators who swoon with rapture each time the exploited in the colonies take up arms against their masters, and who cannot help seeing these uprisings as the epitome of Revolution. . . . Wherever there is a conflict they always see Good fighting Evil, 'total revolution' versus 'total reaction.' . . . Revolutionary criticism begins beyond good and evil; it is rooted in history and operates on the totality of the existing world. In no case can it applaud a belligerent *state* or support the bureaucracy of an exploitive state in the process of formation. . . . It is obviously impossible at present to seek a *revolutionary* solution to the Vietnam war. It is first of all necessary to put an end to the American aggression in order to allow the real social struggle in Vietnam to develop in a *natural way;* i.e. to allow the Vietnamese workers and peasants to rediscover their enemies at home: the bureaucracy of the North and the propertied and ruling strata of the South. Once the Americans withdraw, the Stalinist bureaucracy will seize control of the whole country — there's no getting around this. . . . The point is not to give unconditional (or even conditional) support to the Vietcong, but to struggle consistently and uncompromisingly against American imperialism." (*SI Anthology*, pp. 195-196, 203 [Revised Edition pp. 252-253, 262].)

If you do decide to choose a lesser evil, admit it; don't add to the confusion by whitewashing your choice or demonizing the enemy. If anything, it's better to do the opposite: to play devil's advocate and neutralize compulsive polemical delirium by calmly examining the strong points of the opposing position and the weaknesses in your own. "A very popular error: having the courage of one's convictions; the point is to have the courage for an *attack* on one's convictions!" (Nietzsche).

Combine modesty with audacity. Remember that if you happen to accomplish anything it is on the foundation of the efforts of countless others, many of whom have faced horrors that would make you or me crumple into submission. But don't forget that what you say can make a difference: within a world of pacified spectators even a little autonomous expression will stand out.

Since there are no longer any material obstacles to inaugurating a classless society, the problem has been essentially reduced to a question of consciousness: the only thing that really stands in the way is people's unawareness of their own collective power. (Physical repression is effective against radical minorities only so long as social conditioning keeps the rest of the population docile.) Hence a large element of radical practice is *negative:* attacking the various forms of false consciousness that prevent people from realizing their positive potentialities.

The insurrectionary style
Both Marx and the situationists have often been ignorantly denounced for such negativity, because they concentrated primarily on critical clarification and deliberately avoided promoting any positive ideology to which people could passively cling. Because Marx pointed out how capitalism

reduces our lives to an economic rat-race, "idealistic" apologists for this state of affairs accuse *him* of "reducing life to materialistic concerns" — as if the whole point of Marx's work was not to help us get beyond our economic slavery so that our more creative potentials can flower. "To call on people to give up their illusions about their condition is to call on them to give up a condition that requires illusions. . . . Criticism plucks the imaginary flowers from the chain not in order that man shall continue to bear that chain without fantasy or consolation, but so that he will throw off the chain and pluck the living flower" ("Introduction to a Critique of Hegel's Philosophy of Right").

Accurately expressing a key issue often has a surprisingly powerful effect. Bringing things out into the open forces people to stop hedging their bets and take a position. Like the dexterous butcher in the Taoist fable whose knife never needed sharpening because he always cut between the joints, the most effective radical polarization comes not from strident protest, but from simply revealing the divisions that already exist, elucidating the different tendencies, contradictions, choices. Much of the situationists' impact stemmed from the fact that they articulated things that most people had already experienced but were unable or afraid to express until someone else broke the ice. ("Our ideas are in everybody's mind.")

If some situationist texts nevertheless seem difficult at first, this is because their dialectical structure goes against the grain of our conditioning. When this conditioning is broken they don't seem so obscure (they were the source of some of the most popular May 1968 graffiti). Many academic spectators have floundered around trying unsuccessfully to resolve the various "contradictory" descriptions of the spectacle in *The Society of the Spectacle* into some single, "scientifically consistent" definition; but anyone engaged in contesting this society will find Debord's examination of it from different angles eminently clear and useful, and come to appreciate the fact that he never wastes a word in academic inanities or pointless expressions of outrage.

The dialectical method that runs from Hegel and Marx to the situationists is not a magic formula for churning out correct predictions, it is a tool for grappling with the dynamic processes of social change. It reminds us that social concepts are not eternal; that they contain their own contradictions, interacting with and transforming each other, even into their opposites; that what is true or progressive in one context may become false or regressive in another.[3]

---

3   "In its mystified form, dialectics became the fashion in Germany because it seemed to transfigure and glorify the existing state of things. In its rational form it is a scandal and abomination to bourgeois society and its doctrinaire professors, because in comprehending the existing state of things it simultaneously recognizes the negation of that state, its inevitable breaking up; because it sees the fluid movement of every historically developed social form, and therefore takes into account its transience as well as its momentary existence; because it lets nothing impose on it, and is in its essence critical and revolutionary." (Marx, *Capital*.)

The split between Marxism and anarchism crippled both sides. The anarchists rightly criticized the authoritarian and narrowly economistic tendencies in Marxism, but they generally did so in an undialectical, moralistic, ahistorical manner, contraposing various absolute dualisms (Freedom versus Authority, Individualism versus Collectivism, Centralization versus Decentralization, etc.) and leaving Marx and a few of the more radical Marxists with a virtual monopoly on coherent dialectical analysis — until the situationists finally brought the libertarian and dialectical aspects back together again. On the merits and flaws of Marxism and anarchism see *The*

A dialectical text may require careful study, but each new reading brings new discoveries. Even if it influences only a few people directly, it tends to influence them so profoundly that many of them end up influencing others in the same way, leading to a qualitative chain reaction. The nondialectical language of leftist propaganda is easier to understand, but its effect is usually superficial and ephemeral; offering no challenge, it soon ends up boring even the stupefied spectators for whom it is designed.

As Debord put it in his last film, those who find what he says too difficult would do better to blame their own ignorance and passivity, and the schools and society that have made them that way, than to complain about his obscurity. Those who don't have enough initiative to reread crucial texts or to do a little exploration or a little experimentation for themselves are unlikely to accomplish anything if they are spoonfed by someone else.

Radical film

Debord is in fact virtually the only person who has made a truly dialectical and antispectacular use of film. Although would-be radical filmmakers often give lip service to Brechtian "distanciation" — the notion of encouraging spectators to think and act for themselves rather than sucking them into passive identification with hero or plot — most radical films still play to the audience as if it were made up of morons. The dimwitted protagonist gradually "discovers oppression" and becomes "radicalized" to the point where he is ready to become a fervent supporter of "progressive" politicians or a loyal militant in some bureaucratic leftist group. Distanciation is limited to a few

---

Society of the Spectacle §§78-94.

token gimmicks that allow the spectator to think: "Ah, a Brechtian touch! What a clever fellow that filmmaker is! And how clever am I to recognize such subtleties!" The radical message is usually so banal that it is obvious to virtually anyone who would ever go to see such a film in the first place; but the spectator gets the gratifying impression that *other* people might be brought up to his level of awareness if only they could be got to see it.

If the spectator has any uneasiness about the quality of what he is consuming, it is assuaged by the critics, whose main function is to read profound radical meanings into practically any film. As with the Emperor's New Clothes, no one is likely to admit that he wasn't aware of these supposed meanings until informed of them, for fear that this would reveal him as less sophisticated than the rest of the audience.

Certain films may help expose some deplorable condition or convey some sense of the feel of a radical situation. But there is little point in presenting images of a struggle if both the images and the struggle are not criticized. Spectators sometimes complain that a film portrays some social category (e.g. women) inaccurately. This may be true insofar as the film reproduces certain false stereotypes; but the usually implied alternative — that the filmmaker "should have presented images of women struggling against oppression" — would in most cases be equally false to reality. Women (like men or any other oppressed group) have in fact usually been passive and submissive — that's precisely the problem we have to face. Catering to people's self-satisfaction by presenting spectacles of triumphant radical heroism only reinforces this bondage.

Oppressionism versus playfulness

To rely on oppressive conditions to radicalize people is unwise; to intentionally worsen them in order to accelerate this process is unacceptable. The repression of certain radical projects may incidentally expose the absurdity of the ruling order; but such projects should be worthwhile for their own sake — they lose their credibility if they are merely pretexts designed to provoke repression. Even in the most "privileged" milieus there are usually more than enough problems without needing to add to them. The point is to reveal the *contrast* between present conditions and present *possibilities;* to give people enough taste of real life that they'll want more.

Leftists often imply that a lot of simplification, exaggeration and repetition is necessary in order to counteract all the ruling propaganda in the other direction. This is like saying that a boxer who has been made groggy by a right hook will be restored to lucidity by a left hook.

People's consciousness is not "raised" by burying them under an avalanche of horror stories, or even under an avalanche of information. Information that is not critically assimilated and used is soon forgotten. Mental as well as physical health requires some balance between what we take in and what we do with it. It may sometimes be necessary to force complacent people to face some outrage they are unaware of, but even in such cases harping on the same thing ad nauseam usually accomplishes nothing more than driving them to escape to less boring and depressing spectacles.

One of the main things that keeps us from understanding our situation is the spectacle of other people's apparent happiness, which makes us see our own unhappiness as a shameful sign of failure. But an omnipresent spectacle of misery also keeps us from seeing our positive potentials. The constant broadcasting of delirious ideas and nauseating atrocities paralyzes us, turns us into paranoids and compulsive cynics.

Strident leftist propaganda, fixating on the insidiousness and loathsomeness of "oppressors," often feeds this delirium, appealing to the most morbid and mean-spirited side of people. If we get caught up in brooding on evils, if we let the sickness and ugliness of this society pervade even our rebellion against it, we forget what we are fighting for and end up losing the very capacity to love, to create, to enjoy.

The best "radical art" cuts both ways. If it attacks the alienation of modern life, it simultaneously reminds us of the poetic potentialities hidden within it. Rather than rein-forcing our tendency to wallow in self-pity, it encourages our resilience, enables us to laugh at our own troubles as well as at the asininities of the forces of "order." Some of the old IWW songs and comic strips are good examples, even if the IWW ideology is by now a bit musty. Or the ironic, bittersweet songs of Brecht and Weill. The hilarity of *The Good Soldier Svejk* is probably a more effective antidote to war than the moral outrage of the typical antiwar tract.

Nothing undermines authority like holding it up to ridicule. The most effective argument against a repressive regime is not that it is evil, but that it is silly. The protagonists of Albert Cossery's novel *La violence et la dérision*, living under a Middle-Eastern dictatorship, plaster the walls of the capital with an official-looking poster that praises the dictator to such a preposterous degree that he becomes a laughingstock and is forced to resign out of embarrassment. Cosséry's pranksters are apolitical and their success is perhaps too good to be true, but somewhat similar parodies have been used with more radical aims.[4] At demonstrations in Italy in the 1970s the Metropolitan Indians (inspired perhaps by the opening chapter of Lewis Carroll's *Sylvie and Bruno:* "Less Bread! More Taxes!") carried banners and chanted slogans such as "Power to the Bosses!" and "More work! Less pay!" Everyone recognized the irony, but it was harder to dismiss with the usual pigeonholing.

Humor is a healthy antidote to all types of orthodoxy, left as well as right. It's highly contagious and it reminds us not to take ourselves too seriously. But it can easily become a mere safety valve, channeling dissatisfaction into glib, passive cynicism. Spectacle society thrives on delirious reactions against its most delirious aspects. Satirists often have a dependent, love-hate relation with their targets; parodies become indistinguishable from what they are parodying, giving the impression that everything is equally bizarre, meaningless and hopeless.

In a society based on artificially maintained confusion, the first task is not to add to it. Chaotic disruptions usually generate nothing but annoyance or panic, provoking people to support whatever measures the government takes to restore order. A radical intervention may at first seem strange and incomprehensible; but if it has been worked out with sufficient lucidity, people will soon understand it well enough.

---

4   e.g. the Li I-Che coup mentioned on page 304 of Ken Knabb's *Public Secrets*

The Strasbourg scandal

Imagine being at Strasbourg University at the opening of the school year in fall 1966, among the students, faculty and distinguished guests filing into an auditorium to hear a commencement address. You find a little pamphlet placed on each seat. A program? No, something about "the poverty of student life." You idly open it up and start to read: "It is pretty safe to say that the student is the most universally despised creature in France, apart from the policeman and the priest. . . ." You look around and see that everyone else is also reading it, reactions ranging from puzzlement or amusement to shock and outrage. Who is responsible for this? The title page reveals that it is published by the Strasbourg Student Union, but it also refers to "the Situationist International," whatever that might be. . . .

What made the Strasbourg scandal different from some college prank, or from the confused and confusing capers of groups like the Yippies, was that its scandalous form conveyed an equally scandalous content. At a moment when students were being proclaimed as the most radical sector of society, this text was the only one that put things into perspective. But the particular poverties of students just happened to be the point of departure; equally scathing texts could and should be written on the poverty of every other segment of society (preferably by those who know them from inside). Some have in fact been attempted, but none have approached the lucidity and coherence of the situationist pamphlet, so concise yet so comprehensive, so provocative yet so accurate, moving so methodically from a specific situation through increasingly general ramifications that the final chapter presents the most pithy existing summary of the modern revolutionary project. (See *SI Anthology*, pp. 204-212, 319-337 [Revised Edition pp. 263-273, 408-429].)

The situationists never claimed to have single-handedly provoked May 1968 — as they said, they predicted the content of the revolt, not the date or location. But without the Strasbourg scandal and the subsequent agitation by the SI-influenced Enragés group (of which the more well known March 22nd Movement was only a belated and confused imitation) the revolt might never have happened. There was no economic or governmental crisis, no war or racial antagonism destabilizing the country, nor any other particular issue that might have fostered such a revolt. There were more radical worker struggles going on in Italy and England, more militant student struggles in Germany and Japan, more widespread countercultural movements in the United States and the Netherlands. But only in France was there a perspective that tied them all together.

Carefully calculated interventions like the Strasbourg scandal must be distinguished not only from confusionistic disruptions, but also from merely spectacular exposés. As long as social critics confine themselves to contesting this or that detail, the spectacle-spectator relation continually reconstitutes itself: if such critics succeed in discrediting existing political leaders, they themselves often become new stars (Ralph Nader, Noam Chomsky, etc.) whom slightly more aware spectators admiringly rely on for a continuing flow of shocking information that they rarely do anything about. The milder exposés get the audience to root for this or that faction in intragovernmental power struggles; the more sensational ones feed people's morbid curiosity, sucking them into consuming more articles, news programs and docudramas, and into interminable debates about various conspiracy theories. Most such theories are obviously nothing but delirious reflections of the lack of critical historical sense produced by the modern spectacle, desperate attempts to find some coherent meaning in an increasingly incoherent and absurd society. In any case, as long as things remain on the spectacular terrain it hardly matters whether any of these theories are true: *those who keep watching to see what comes next never affect what comes next.*

Certain revelations are more interesting because they not only open up significant issues to public debate, but do so in a manner that draws lots of people into the game. A charming example is the 1963 "Spies for Peace" scandal in England, in which a few unknown persons publicized the location of a secret bomb shelter reserved for members of the government. The more vehemently the government threatened to prosecute anyone who reproduced this "state secret" information which was no longer secret from anyone, the more creatively and playfully it was disseminated by thousands of groups and individuals (who also proceeded to discover and invade several other secret shelters). Not only did the asininity of the government and the insanity of the nuclear war spectacle became evident to everyone, the spontaneous human chain reaction provided a taste of a quite different social potential.

The poverty of electoral politics

"Since 1814 no Liberal government had come in except by violence. Cánovas was too intelligent not to see the inconvenience and the danger of that. He therefore arranged that Conservative governments should be succeeded regularly by Liberal governments. The plan he followed was, whenever an economic crisis or a serious strike came along, to resign and let the Liberals deal with it. This explains why most of the repressive legislation passed during the rest of the century was passed by them."

—Gerald Brenan, *The Spanish Labyrinth*

The best argument in favor of radical electoral politics was made by Eugene Debs, the American socialist leader who in 1920 received nearly a million votes for president while in prison for opposing World War I: "If the people don't know enough to know who to vote for, they're not going to know who to shoot at." On the other hand, the workers during the 1918-19 German revolution were confused about who to shoot at precisely by the presence of "socialist" leaders in the government who were working overtime to repress the revolution.

In itself, voting is of no great significance one way or the other (those who make a big deal about refusing to vote are only revealing their own fetishism). The problem is that it tends to lull people into relying on others to act for them, distracting them from more significant possibilities. A few people who take some creative initiative (think of the first civil rights sit-ins) may ultimately have a far greater effect than if they had put their energy into campaigning for lesser-evil politicians. At best, legislators rarely do more than what they have been forced to do by popular movements. A conservative regime under pressure from independent radical movements often concedes more than a liberal regime that knows it can count on radical support. If people invariably rally to lesser evils, all the rulers have to do in any situation that threatens their power is to conjure up a threat of some greater evil.

Even in the rare case when a "radical" politician has a realistic chance of winning an election, all the tedious campaign efforts of thousands of people may go down the drain in one day because of some trivial scandal discovered in his personal life, or because he inadvertently says something intelligent. If he manages to avoid these pitfalls and it looks like he might win, he tends to evade controversial issues for fear of antagonizing swing voters. If he actually gets elected he is almost never in a position to implement the reforms he has promised, except perhaps after years of wheeling and dealing with his new colleagues; which gives him a good excuse to see his first priority as making whatever compromises are necessary to keep himself in office indefinitely. Hobnobbing with the rich and powerful, he develops new interests and new tastes, which he justifies by telling himself that he deserves a few perks after all his years of working for good causes. Worst of all, if he does eventually manage to get a few "progressive" measures passed, this exceptional and usually trivial success is held up as evidence of the value of relying on electoral politics, luring many more people into wasting their energy on similar campaigns to come.

As one of the May 1968 graffiti put it, "It's painful to submit to our bosses; it's even more stupid to choose them!"

Referendums on particular issues are less susceptible to the precariousness of personalities; but the results are often no better since the issues tend to be posed very simplistically, and any measure that threatens powerful interests can usually be defeated by the influence of money and mass media.

Local elections sometimes offer people a more realistic chance to affect policies and keep tabs on elected officials. But even the most enlightened communities cannot insulate themselves from the deterioration of the rest of the world. If a city manages to preserve desirable cultural or environmental features, these very advantages put it under increasing economic pressure. The fact that human values have been given precedence over property values ultimately causes enormous increases in the latter (more people will want to invest or move there). Sooner or later this property-value increase overpowers the human values: local policies are overruled by high courts or by state or national governments, outside money is poured into municipal elections, city officials are bribed, residential neighborhoods are demolished to make room for highrises and freeways, rents skyrocket, the poorer classes are forced out (including the diverse ethnic groups and artistic bohemians who contributed to the city's original liveliness and appeal), and all that remains of the earlier community are a few isolated sites of "historical interest" for tourist consumption.

Reforms and alternative institutions

Still, "acting locally" may be a good place to start. People who feel that the global situation is hopeless or incomprehensible may nevertheless see a chance to affect some specific local matter. Block clubs, co-ops, switchboards, study groups, alternative schools, free health clinics, community theaters, neighborhood newspapers, public-access radio and television stations and many other kinds of alternative institutions are worthwhile for their own sake, and if they are sufficiently participatory they may lead to broader movements. Even if they don't last very long, they provide a temporary terrain for radical experimentation.

But always within limits. Capitalism was able to develop gradually within feudal society, so that by the time the capitalist revolution cast off the last vestiges of feudalism, most of the mechanisms of the new bourgeois order were already firmly in place. An anticapitalist revolution, in contrast, cannot really build its new society "within the shell of the old." Capitalism is far more flexible and all-pervading than was feudalism, and tends to coopt any oppositional organization.

Nineteenth-century radical theorists could still see enough surviving remnants of traditional communal forms to suppose that, once the overarching exploitive structure was eliminated, they might be revived and expanded to form the foundation of a new society. But the global penetration of spectacular capitalism in the present century has destroyed virtually all forms of popular control and direct human interaction. Even the more modern efforts of the sixties counterculture have long been integrated into the system. Co-ops, crafts, organic farming and other marginal enterprises may produce better quality goods under better working conditions, but those goods still have to function as commodities on the market. The few successful ventures tend to evolve into ordinary businesses, with the founding members gradually assuming an ownership or managerial role over the newer workers and dealing with all sorts of routine commercial and bureaucratic matters that have nothing to do with "preparing the ground for a new society."

The longer an alternative institution lasts, the more it tends to lose its volunteer, experimental, nothing-to-lose character. Permanent paid staffs develop a vested interest in the status quo and avoid rocking the boat for fear of offending supporters or losing their government or foundation funding. Alternative institutions also tend to demand too much of the limited free time people have, bogging them down, robbing them of the energy and imagination to confront more general issues. After a brief period of participation most people get burned out, leaving the work to the dutiful types or to leftists trying to make an ideological point. It may sound nice to hear about people forming block clubs, etc., but unless a real local emergency comes up you may not *want* to attend interminable meetings to listen to your neighbors' complaints, or otherwise commit yourself to matters you don't really care about.

In the name of realism, reformists limit themselves to pursuing "winnable" objectives, yet even when they win some little adjustment in the system it is usually offset by some other development at another level. This doesn't mean that reforms are irrelevant, merely that they are insufficient. We have to keep resisting particular evils, but we also have to recognize that the system will keep generating new ones until we put an end to it. To suppose that a series of reforms will eventually add up to a qualitative change is like thinking we can get across a ten-foot chasm by a series of one-foot hops.

People tend to assume that because revolution involves much greater change than reforms, it must be more difficult to bring about. In the long run it may actually be easier, because in one stroke it cuts through so many petty complications and arouses a much greater enthusiasm. At a certain point it becomes more practical to start fresh than to keep trying to replaster a rotten structure.

Meanwhile, until a revolutionary situation enables us to be truly constructive, the best we can do is be *creatively negative* — concentrating on critical clarification, leaving people to pursue whatever positive projects may appeal to them but without the illusion that a new society is being "built" by the gradual accumulation of such projects.

Purely negative projects (e.g. abolition of laws against drug use, consensual sex and other victimless crimes) have the advantage of simplicity, immediately benefiting virtually everyone (except for that symbiotic duo, organized crime and the crime-control industry) while requiring little if any followup work once they are successful. On the other hand, they provide little opportunity for creative participation.

The best projects are those that are worthwhile for their own sake while simultaneously containing an implicit challenge to some fundamental aspect of the system; projects that enable people to participate in significant issues according to their own degree of interest, while tending to open the way to more radical possibilities.

Less interesting, but still worthwhile, are demands for improved conditions or more equal rights. Even if such projects are not in themselves very participatory, they may remove impediments to participation.

Least desirable are mere zero-sum struggles, where one group's gain is another's loss.

Even in the latter case the point is not to tell people what they should do, but to get them to realize what they are doing. If they are promoting some issue in order to recruit people, it is appropriate to expose their manipulative motives. If they believe they are contributing to radical change, it may be useful to show them how their activity is actually reinforcing the system in some way. But if they are really interested in their project for its own sake, let them go for it.

Even if we disagree with their priorities (fundraising for the opera, say, while the streets are filled with homeless people) we should be wary of any strategy that merely appeals to people's guilt, not only because such appeals generally have a negligible effect but because such moralism represses healthy positive aspirations. To refrain from contesting "quality of life" issues because the system continues to present us with survival emergencies is to submit to a blackmail that no longer has any justification. "Bread and roses" are no longer mutually exclusive.[5]

"Quality of life" projects are in fact often more inspiring than routine political and economic demands because they awaken people to richer perspectives. Paul Goodman's books are full of imaginative and often amusing examples. If his proposals are "reformist," they are so in a lively, provocative way that provides a refreshing contrast to the cringing defensive posture of most present-day reformists, who confine themselves to reacting to the reactionaries' agenda. ("We agree that it is essential to create jobs, fight crime, keep our country strong; but

---

5   "What surfaced this spring in Zurich as a demonstration against the closing of a youth center has crept across Switzerland, feeding on the restlessness of a young generation anxious to break out of what they see as a suffocating society. 'We don't want a world where the guarantee of not dying of hunger is paid for by the certainty of dying of boredom,' proclaim banners and spray-painted storefronts in Lausanne." (*Christian Science Monitor,* 28 October 1980.) The slogan is from Vaneigem's *The Revolution of Everyday Life.*

moderate methods will accomplish this better than the conservatives' extremist proposals.")

Other things being equal, it makes sense to concentrate one's energy on issues that are not already receiving public attention; and to prefer projects that can be done cleanly and directly, as opposed to those that require compromises, such as working through government agencies. Even if such compromises don't seem too serious, they set a bad precedent. Reliance on the state almost always backfires (commissions designed to root out bureaucratic corruption themselves develop into new corrupt bureaucracies; laws designed to thwart armed reactionary groups end up being used primarily to harass unarmed radicals).

The system is able to kill two birds with one stone by maneuvering its opponents into offering "constructive solutions" to its own crises. It in fact needs a certain amount of opposition to warn it of problems, to force it to rationalize itself, to enable it to test its instruments of control, and to provide excuses to impose new forms of control. Emergency measures imperceptibly become standard procedures as regulations that might ordinarily be resisted are introduced during situations of panic. The slow, steady rape of the human personality by all the institutions of alienated society, from school and factory to advertising and urbanism, is made to seem normal as the spectacle focuses obsessively on sensational individual crimes, manipulating people into law-and-order hysteria.

Political correctness, or equal opportunity alienation
Above all, the system thrives when it can deflect social contestation into squabbles over privileged positions within it.

This is a particularly thorny area. All social inequalities need to be challenged, not only because they are unfair, but because as long as they remain they can be used to divide people. But attaining equal wage slavery or equal opportunity to become a bureaucrat or a capitalist hardly amounts to any victory over bureaucratic capitalism.

It is both natural and necessary that people defend their own interests; but if they try do so by identifying too exclusively with some particular social group they tend to lose sight of the larger picture. As increasingly fragmented categories scramble over the crumbs allotted to them, they get caught up in petty mutual-blame games and the notion of abolishing the whole hierarchical structure is forgotten. People who are normally quick to denounce the slightest hint of derogatory stereotyping get carried away into lumping all men or all whites as "oppressors," then wonder why they run up against such powerful backlashes among the vast majority of the latter, who are quite aware that they have little real power over their own lives, much less over anyone else's.

Aside from the reactionary demagogues (who are pleasantly surprised to find "progressives" providing them with such easy targets for ridicule) the only people who actually benefit from these internecine squabbles are a few careerists struggling for bureaucratic posts, government grants, academic tenure, publishing contracts, commercial clienteles or political constituencies at a time when there is increasingly limited space at the trough. Sniffing out "political incorrectness" enables them to bash rivals and critics and reinforce their own positions as recognized specialists or spokespeople of their particular fragment. The various oppressed groups that are foolish enough to accept such spokespeople get nothing but the bittersweet thrill of self-righteous resentment and a ludicrous official terminology reminiscent of Orwell's Newspeak.[6]

There is a crucial, though sometimes subtle, distinction between fighting social evils and *feeding* on them. People are not empowered by being encouraged to wallow in their own victimhood. Individual autonomy is not developed by taking refuge in some group identity. Equal intelligence is not demonstrated by dismissing logical reasoning as a "typical white male tactic." Radical dialogue is not fostered by harassing people who don't conform to some political orthodoxy, much less by striving to get such orthodoxy legally enforced.

Nor is history made by rewriting it. We do need to free ourselves from uncritical respect for the past and to become aware of the ways it has been distorted. But we have to recognize that despite our disapproval of past prejudices and injustices, it is unlikely that we would have done any better had we ourselves lived under the same conditions. Applying present-day standards retroactively (smugly correcting earlier authors every time they use the formerly conventional masculine forms, or trying to censor *Huckleberry Finn* because Huck doesn't refer to Jim as a "person of color") only reinforces the historical ignorance that the modern spectacle has been so successful in fostering.

---

6   For some hilarious examples see Henry Beard and Christopher Cerf's *The Official Politically Correct Dictionary and Handbook* (Villard, 1992): it's often hard to tell which of the Correctspeak terms are satirical and which have actually been seriously proposed or even officially adopted and enforced. The only antidote to such delirium is a lot of healthy guffaws.

Drawbacks of moralism and simplistic extremism

A lot of this nonsense stems from the false assumption that being radical implies living up to some moral "principle" — as if no one could work for peace without being a total pacifist, or advocate the abolition of capitalism without giving away all their money. Most people have too much common sense to actually follow such simplistic ideals, but they often feel vaguely guilty that they don't. This guilt paralyzes them and makes them more susceptible to blackmail by leftist manipulators (who tell us that if we don't have the courage to martyrize ourselves, we must uncritically support those who do). Or they try to repress their guilt by disparaging others who seem even more compromised: a manual laborer may take pride in not selling out mentally like a professor; who perhaps feels superior to an ad designer; who may in turn look down on someone who works in the arms industry. . . .

Turning social problems into personal moral issues deflects attention from their potential solution. Trying to change social conditions by charity is like trying to raise the sea level by dumping buckets of water in the ocean. Even if some good is accomplished by altruistic actions, to rely on them as a general strategy is futile because they will always be the exception. Most people naturally look out first for themselves and for those closest to them. One of the merits of the situationists was to have cut through the traditional leftist appeal to guilt and self-sacrifice by stressing that the primary reason to make a revolution is for ourselves.

"Going to the people" in order to "serve" or "organize" or "radicalize" them usually leads to manipulation and often meets with apathy or hostility. The example of others' independent actions is a far stronger and healthier means of inspiration. Once people begin to act on their own they are in a better position to exchange experiences, to collaborate on equal terms and, if necessary, to *ask* for specific assistance. And when they win their own freedom it's much harder to take it back from them. One of the May 1968 graffitists wrote: "I'm not a servant of the people (much less of their self-appointed leaders) — let the people serve themselves." Another put it even more succinctly: "Don't liberate me — I'll take care of that."

A total critique means that everything is called into question, not that everything must be totally opposed. Radicals often forget this and get caught up in outbidding each other with increasingly extremist assertions, implying that any compromise amounts to selling out or even that any enjoyment amounts to complicity with the system. Actually, being "for" or "against" some political position is just as easy, and usually just as meaningless, as being for or against some sports team. Those who proudly proclaim their "total opposition" to all compromise, all authority, all organization, all theory, all technology, etc., usually turn out to have no *revolutionary* perspective whatsoever — no practical conception of how the present system might be overthrown or how a postrevolutionary society might work. Some even attempt to justify this lack by declaring that a mere revolution could never be radical enough to satisfy their eternal ontological rebelliousness.

Such all-or-nothing bombast may temporarily impress a few spectators, but its ultimate effect is simply to make people blasé. Sooner or later the contradictions and hypocrisies lead to disillusionment and resignation. Projecting their own disappointed delusions onto the world, the former extremists conclude that all radical change is hopeless and repress the whole experience; or perhaps even flip to some equally silly reactionary position.

If every radical had to be a Durruti we might as well forget it and devote ourselves to more realizable concerns. But being radical does not mean being the most extreme. In its original sense it simply means going to the root. The reason it is necessary to strive for the abolition of capitalism and the state is not because this is the most extreme goal imaginable, but because it has unfortunately become evident that nothing less will do.

We need to find out what is both necessary and sufficient; to seek projects that we are actually capable of doing and realistically likely to do. Anything beyond this is just hot air. Many of the oldest and still most effective radical tactics — debates, critiques, boycotts, strikes, sit-ins, workers councils — caught on precisely because they are at once simple, relatively safe, widely applicable, and open-ended enough to lead to broader possibilities.

Simplistic extremism naturally seeks the most extremist foil for itself. If all problems can be attributed to a sinister clique of "total fascists," everything else will seem comfortingly progressive by comparison. Meanwhile the actual forms of modern domination, which are usually more subtle, proceed unnoticed and unopposed.

Fixating on reactionaries only reinforces them, makes them seem more powerful and more fascinating. "It matters little if our opponents mock us or insult us, if they represent us as clowns or criminals; the essential thing is that they talk of us, preoccupy themselves with us" (Hitler). Reich pointed out that "by drilling people to hate the police one only strengthens police authority and invests it with mystic power in the eyes of the poor and the helpless. The strong are hated but also feared and envied and followed. This fear and envy felt by the 'have-nots' accounts for a portion of the political reactionaries' power. One of the main objectives of the rational struggle for freedom is to disarm reactionaries by exposing the illu-sionary character of their power" (*People in Trouble*).

The main problem with compromising is not so much moral as practical: it's difficult to attack something when we ourselves are implicated in it. We hedge our critiques lest others criticize us in turn. It becomes harder to think big, to act boldly. As has often been noted, many of the German people acquiesced to Nazi oppression because it began fairly gradually and was at first directed mainly at unpopular minorities (Jews, Gypsies, Commu-nists, homosexuals); by the time it began affecting the general population, they had become incapable of doing anything about it.

In hindsight it's easy to condemn those who capitu-lated to fascism or Stalinism, but it's unlikely that most of us would have done any better had we been in the same position. In our daydreams, picturing ourself as a dramatic personage faced with a clear-cut choice in front of an appreciative audience, we imagine that we would have no trouble making the right decision. But the situations we actually face are usually more complex and obscure. It's not always easy to know where to draw the line.

The point is to draw it *somewhere,* stop worrying about guilt and blame and self-justification, and take the offen-sive.

Advantages of boldness

This spirit is well exemplified by those Italian workers who have gone on strike without making any demands whatsoever. Such strikes are not only more interesting than the usual bureaucratic union negotiations, they may even be more effective: the bosses, uncertain of how far they have to go, frequently end up offering much more than the strikers would have dared to demand. The latter can then decide on their next move without having committed themselves to anything in return.

A defensive reaction against this or that social symptom at best wins some temporary concession on the specific issue. Aggressive agitation that refuses to limit itself exerts far more pressure. Faced with widespread, unpredictable movements like the sixties counterculture or the May 1968 revolt — movements calling everything in question, generating autonomous contestations on many fronts, threatening to spread throughout the whole society and too vast to be controlled by cooptable leaders — rulers hasten to clean up their image, pass reforms, raise wages, release prisoners, declare amnesties, initiate peace talks — anything in the hope of preempting the movement and reestablishing their control. (The sheer unmanageability of the American counterculture, which was spreading deeply into the army itself, probably played as great a role as the explicit antiwar movement in forcing the end of the Vietnam war.)

The side that takes the initiative defines the terms of the struggle. As long as it keeps innovating, it also retains the element of surprise. "Boldness is virtually a creative power. . . . Whenever boldness meets hesitation it already has a significant advantage because the very state of hesitation implies a loss of equilibrium. It is only when it encounters cautious foresight that it is at a disadvantage"

(Clausewitz, *On War*). But cautious foresight is quite rare among those who run this society. Most of the system's processes of commodification, spectacularization and hierarchization are blind and automatic: merchants, media and leaders merely follow their natural tendencies to make money or grab audiences or recruit followers.

Spectacle society is often the victim of its own falsifications. As each level of bureaucracy tries to cover for itself with padded statistics, as each "information source" outbids the others with more sensational stories, and as competing states, governmental departments and private companies each launch their own independent disinformation operations (see chapters 16 and 30 of Debord's *Comments on the Society of the Spectacle*), even the exceptional ruler who may have some lucidity has a hard time finding out what is really happening. As Debord observes elsewhere in the same book, a state that ends up repressing its own historical knowledge can no longer conduct itself strategically.

Advantages and limits of nonviolence

"The whole history of the progress of human liberty shows that all concessions yet made to her august claims have been born of struggle. . . . If there is no struggle there is no progress. Those who profess to favor freedom and yet deprecate agitation, are men who want crops without plowing up the ground. They want rain without thunder and lightning. They want the ocean without the awful roar of its many waters. The struggle may be a moral one; or it may be a physical one; or it may be both moral and physical, but it must be a struggle. Power concedes nothing without a demand. It never did and it never will."

—Frederick Douglass

Anyone with any knowledge of history is aware that societies do not change without stubborn and often savage resistance by those in power. If our ancestors had not resorted to violent revolt, most of those who now self-righteously deplore it would still be serfs or slaves.

The routine functioning of this society is far more violent than any reaction against it could ever be. Imagine the outrage that would greet a radical movement that executed 20,000 opponents; that's a conservative estimate of the number of children that the present system allows to starve to death *each day*. Vacillations and compromises allow this ongoing violence to drag on indefinitely, ultimately causing a thousand times more suffering than a single decisive revolution.

Fortunately a modern, genuinely majority revolution would have relatively little need for violence except to neutralize those elements of the ruling minority who try to violently maintain their own power.

Violence is not only undesirable in itself, it generates panic (and thus manipulability) and promotes militaristic (and thus hierarchical) organization. Nonviolence entails more open and democratic organization; it tends to foster composure and compassion and to break the miserable cycle of hatred and revenge.

But we have to avoid making a fetish out of it. The common retort, "How can you work for peace with violent methods?" is no more logical than it would be to tell a drowning man that if he wants to get to dry land he must avoid touching water. Striving to resolve "misunderstand-ings" through dialogue, pacifists forget that some problems are based on objective conflicts of interest. They tend to underestimate the malice of enemies while exaggerating their own guilt, berating themselves even for their "violent feelings." The seemingly personal practice of "bearing witness" actually reduces the activist to a passive object, "another person for peace" who (like a soldier) puts her body on the line while abdicating personal investigation or experimentation. Those who want to undermine the notion of war as exciting and heroic must get beyond such a cringing, beggarly notion of peace. Defining their objective as survival, peace activists have had little to say to those who are fascinated by global annihilation precisely because they are sick of an everyday life reduced to mere survival, who see war not as a threat but as a welcome deliverance from a life of boredom and constant petty anxiety.

Sensing that their purism would not hold up under the test of reality, pacifists usually remain deliberately ignorant about past and present social struggles. Though often capable of intensive study and stoic self-discipline in their personal spiritual practices, they seem to feel that a *Reader's Digest* level of historical and strategical knowledge will suffice for their ventures into "social engagement." Like someone hoping to eliminate injurious falls by abolishing the law of gravity, they find it simpler to envision a never-ending moral struggle against "greed," "hatred," "igno-rance," "bigotry," than to challenge the specific social structures that actually reinforce such qualities. If pressed, they sometimes complain that radical contestation is a very stressful terrain. It is indeed, but this is a strange objection to hear from those whose spiritual practices claim to enable people to confront problems with detachment and equanimity.

There's a wonderful moment in *Uncle Tom's Cabin*: As a Quaker family is helping some slaves escape to Canada, a Southern slave catcher appears. One of the Quakers points a shotgun at him and says, "Friend, thee isn't wanted here." I think that's just the right tone: not caught up in hatred, or even contempt, but ready to do what is necessary in a given situation.

Reactions against oppressors are understandable, but those who get too caught up in them risk becoming mentally as well as materially enslaved, chained to their masters by "bonds of hate." Hatred of bosses is partly a projection of people's self-hatred for all the humiliations and compromises they have accepted, stemming from their secret awareness that bosses ultimately exist only because the bossed put up with them. Even if there is some tendency for the scum to rise to the top, most people in positions of power don't act much differently than would anyone else who happened to find themselves in the same position, with the same new interests, temptations and fears.

Vigorous retaliation may teach enemy forces to respect you, but it also tends to perpetuate antagonisms. Forgiveness sometimes wins over enemies, but in other cases it simply gives them a chance to recover and strike again. It's not always easy to determine which policy is best in which circumstances. People who have suffered under particularly vicious regimes naturally want to see the perpetrators punished; but too much revenge sends a message to other present and future oppressors that they may as well fight to the death since they have nothing to lose.

But most people, even those who have been most blamably complicitous with the system, will tend to go whichever way the wind blows. The best defense against counterrevolution is not to be preoccupied with sniffing out people's past offenses or potential future betrayals, but to deepen the insurgence to the point that everyone is drawn in.

Chapter 3: Climaxes

> "As soon as the relations of exploitation and the violence that underlies them are no longer concealed by the mystical veil, there is a break-through, a moment of clarity, the struggle against alienation is suddenly revealed as a ruthless hand-to-hand fight with naked power, power exposed in its brute force and its weakness, a vulnerable giant . . . . sublime moment when the complexity of the world becomes tangible, transparent, within everyone's grasp."
>
> —Raoul Vaneigem, *Basic Banalities* (*SI Anthology,* p. 93 [Revised Edition p. 121])

Causes of social breakthroughs

It's hard to generalize about the immediate causes of radical breakthroughs. There have always been plenty of good reasons to revolt, and sooner or later instabilities will arise where something has to give. But why at one moment and not another? Revolts have often occurred during periods of social improvement, while worse conditions have been endured with resignation. If some have been provoked by sheer desperation, others have been touched off by relatively trivial incidents. Grievances that have been patiently accepted as long as they seemed inevitable may suddenly seem intolerable once it appears possible to remove them. The meanness of some repressive measure or the asininity of some bureaucratic blunder may bring home the absurdity of the system more clearly than a steady accumulation of oppressions.

The system's power is based on people's belief in their powerlessness to oppose it. Normally this belief is well founded (transgress the rules and you are punished). But when for one reason or another enough people begin to ignore the rules that they can do so with impunity, the whole illusion collapses. What was thought to be natural and inevitable is seen to be arbitrary and absurd. "When no one obeys, no one commands."

The problem is how to reach this point. If only a few disobey, they can easily be isolated and repressed. People often fantasize about wonderful things that might be achieved "if only everyone would agree to do such and such all at once." Unfortunately, social movements don't usually work that way. One person with a six-gun can hold off a hundred unarmed people because each one knows that the first six to attack will be killed.

Of course some people may be so infuriated that they attack regardless of risk; and their apparent determination may even save them by convincing those in power that it's wiser to give in peacefully than to be overwhelmed after arousing even more hatred against themselves. But it is obviously preferable not to depend on acts of desperation, but to seek forms of struggle that minimize risk until a movement has spread so far that repression is no longer feasible.

People living under particularly repressive regimes naturally begin by taking advantage of whatever rallying points already exist. In 1978 the Iranian mosques were the only place people could get away with criticizing the Shah's regime. Then the huge demonstrations called by Khomeini at 40-day intervals began providing the safety of numbers. Khomeini thus became recognized as a general symbol of opposition, even by those who were not his followers. But tolerating any leader, even as a mere figurehead, is at best a temporary measure that should be abandoned as soon as more independent action becomes possible — as did those Iranian oil workers who by fall 1978 felt they had enough leverage to strike on days different from those called for by Khomeini.

The Catholic Church in Stalinist Poland played a similarly ambiguous role: the state used the Church to help control the people, but the people also used the Church to help them get around the state.

Fanatical orthodoxy is sometimes the first step toward more radical self-expression. Islamic fundamentalists may be extremely reactionary, but by getting used to taking events in their own hands they complicate any return to "order" and may even, if disillusioned, become genuinely radical — as happened with some of the similarly fanatical Red Guards during the Chinese "Cultural Revolution," when what was originally a mere ploy by Mao to lever out some of his bureaucratic rivals eventually led to uncontrolled insurgency by millions of young people who took his antibureaucratic rhetoric seriously.[1]

Postwar upheavals

If someone proclaimed: "I am the greatest, strongest, noblest, cleverest, and most peace-loving person in the

---

1   On the Cultural Revolution, see *SI Anthology*, pp. 185-194 [Revised Edition pp. 240-251], and Simon Leys's *The Chairman's New Clothes*.

world," he would be considered obnoxious, if not insane. But if he says precisely the same things about his country he is looked upon as an admirably patriotic citizen. Patriotism is extremely seductive because it enables even the most miserable individual to indulge in a vicarious collective narcissism. The natural nostalgic fondness for one's home and surroundings is transformed into a mindless cult of the state. People's fears and resentments are projected onto foreigners while their frustrated aspirations for authentic community are mystically projected onto their own nation, which is seen as somehow essentially wonderful despite all its defects. ("Yes, America has its problems; but what we are fighting for is the *real* America, what America really stands for.") This mystical herd-consciousness becomes almost irresistible during war, smothering virtually all radical tendencies.

Yet patriotism has sometimes played a role in triggering radical struggles (e.g. Hungary 1956). And even wars have sometimes led to revolts in the aftermath. Those who have borne the greatest share of the military burden, supposedly in the name of freedom and democracy, may return home to demand a fairer share for themselves. Seeing historic struggle in action and acquiring the habit of dealing with obstacles by destroying them, they may be less inclined to believe in a changeless status quo.

The dislocations and disillusionments produced by World War I led to uprisings all over Europe. If World War II did not do the same, it was because genuine radicalism had since been destroyed by Stalinism, fascism and reformism; because the victors' rationales for the war, though full of lies as always, were more credible than usual (the defeated enemies were more obvious villains); and because this time the victors had taken care to work out the postwar reestablishment of order in advance (eastern Europe was handed over to Stalin in exchange for his guaranteeing the docility of the French and Italian Communist Parties and his abandonment of the insurgent Greek CP). Nevertheless the global jolt of the war was sufficient to open the way for an autonomous Stalinist revolution in China (which Stalin had not wanted, as this threatened his exclusive domination of the "socialist camp") and to give a new impetus to the anticolonial movements (which the European colonial powers naturally did not want, though they were eventually able to retain the more profitable aspects of their domination through the sort of economic neocolonialism that the United States was already practicing).

Faced with the prospect of a postwar power vacuum, rulers often collaborate with their ostensible enemies in order to repress their own people. At the end of the Franco-German war of 1870-71 the victorious German army helped surround the Paris Commune, enabling the French rulers to crush it more easily. As Stalin's army approached Warsaw in 1944 it called on the people of the city to rise against the Nazi occupiers, then waited outside the city for several days while the Nazis wiped out the thus-exposed independent elements which might later have resisted the imposition of Stalinism. We have recently seen a similar scenario in the de facto Bush-Saddam alliance in the aftermath of the Gulf war, when, after calling on the Iraqi people to rise against Saddam, the American military systematically massacred Iraqi conscripts retreating from Kuwait (who, if they had regained their country, would have been ripe for revolt) while leaving Saddam's elite

Republican Guards intact and free to crush the immense radical uprisings in northern and southern Iraq.[2]

In totalitarian societies the grievances are obvious but revolt is difficult. In "democratic" societies struggles are easier, but the goals are less clear. Controlled largely by subconscious conditioning or by vast, seemingly incomprehensible forces ("the state of the economy") and offered a wide range of apparently free choices, it's difficult for us to grasp our situation. Like a flock of sheep, we're herded in the desired direction, but allowed enough room for individual variations to enable us to preserve an illusion of independence.

Impulses toward vandalism or violent confrontation can often be seen as attempts to break through this frustrating abstractness and come to grips with something concrete.

Just as the first organization of the classical proletariat was preceded, during the end of the eighteenth century and the beginning of the

2   "As Shiites and Kurds battle the regime of Saddam Hussein and Iraqi opposition parties try to patch together a democratic future, the United States finds itself in the awkward position of, in effect, supporting continuing one-party rule in Iraq. US government statements, including those of President Bush, have stressed the desire to see Saddam Hussein overthrown, but not to see Iraq broken apart by civil strife. At the same time, Bush administration officials have insisted that democracy is not currently a viable alternative for Iraq. . . . This may account for the fact that thus far, the administration has refused to meet with Iraqi opposition leaders in exile . . . . 'The Arabs and the US have the same agenda,' says a coalition diplomat. 'We want Iraq in the same borders and Saddam to disappear. But we will accept Saddam in Baghdad in order to have Iraq as one state.' " (*Christian Science Monitor,* 20 March 1991.)

nineteenth, by a period of isolated "criminal" acts aimed at destroying the machines of production that were depriving people of their work, we are presently witnessing the first appearance of a wave of vandalism against the *machines of consumption* that are just as certainly depriving us of our life. In both cases the significance obviously does not lie in the destruction itself, but in the rebelliousness which could potentially develop into a positive project going to the point of reconverting the machines in a way that increases people's real power over their lives. (*SI Anthology,* p. 82 [Revised Edition p. 108].)

(Note that last sentence, incidentally: To point out a symptom of social crisis, or even to defend it as an understandable reaction, does not necessary imply recommending it as a tactic.)

Many other triggers of radical situations could be enumerated. A strike may spread (Russia 1905); popular resistance to some reactionary threat may overflow official bounds (Spain 1936); people may take advantage of token liberalization in order to push further (Hungary 1956, Czechoslovakia 1968); exemplary small group actions may catalyze a mass movement (the early civil rights sit-ins, May 1968); a particular outrage may be seen as the last straw (Watts 1965, Los Angeles 1992); the sudden collapse of a regime may leave a power vacuum (Portugal 1974); some special occasion may bring people together in such numbers that it's impossible to prevent them from expressing their grievances and aspirations (Tiananmen Square 1976 and 1989); etc.

But social crises involve so many imponderables that it is rarely possible to predict them, much less provoke them. In general it seems best to pursue projects we are personally most drawn to, while trying to remain aware enough to quickly recognize significant new developments (dangers, urgent tasks, favorable opportunities) that call for new tactics.

Meanwhile, we can move on to examine some of the crucial stages in radical situations once they do get started.

Effervescence of radical situations

A radical situation is a collective awakening. At one extreme it may involve a few dozen people in a neighborhood or workplace; at the other it shades into a full-fledged revolutionary situation involving millions of people. It's not a matter of numbers, but of open-ended public dialogue and participation. The incident at the beginning of the1964 Free Speech Movement (FSM) is a classic and particularly beautiful example. As police were about to take away an arrested civil rights activist on the university campus in Berkeley, a few students sat down in front of the police car; within a few minutes hundreds of others spontaneously followed their example, surrounding the car so it could not move. For the next 32 hours the car roof was turned into a platform for freewheeling debate. The May 1968 occupation of the Sorbonne created an even more radical situation by drawing in much of the nonstudent Parisian population; the workers' occupation of factories throughout France then turned it into a revolutionary situation.

In such situations people become much more open to new perspectives, readier to question previous assumptions, quicker to see through the usual cons. Every day *some* people go through experiences that lead them to question the meaning of their lives; but during a radical situation practically everyone does so all at once. When the machine grinds to a halt, the cogs themselves begin wondering about their function.

Bosses are ridiculed. Orders are ignored. Separations are broken down. Personal problems are transformed into public issues; public issues that seemed distant and abstract become immediate practical matters. The old order is analyzed, criticized, satirized. People learn more about society in a week than in years of academic "social studies" or leftist "consciousness raising." Long repressed experiences are revived.[3] Everything seems possible — and much more *is* possible. People can hardly believe what they used to put up with in "the old days." Even if the outcome is uncertain, the experience is often seen as worthwhile for its own sake. "If we only have enough time . . ." wrote one May 1968 graffitist; to which a couple others responded: "In any case, no regrets!" and "Already ten days of happiness."

As work comes to a halt, rat-race commuting is

---

3   "I am flabbergasted at the memory people retain of their own revolutionary past. Present events have shaken that memory. Dates never learned at school, songs never sung openly, are recalled in their totality. . . . The noise, the noise, the noise is still ringing in my ears. The horns tooting in joy, the shouting, the slogans, the singing and dancing. The doors of revolution seem open again, after forty-eight years of repression. In that single day everything was replaced in perspective. Nothing was god-given, all was man-made. People could see their misery and their problems in a historical setting. . . . A week has passed, although it already feels like many months. Every hour has been lived to the full. It is already difficult to remember what the papers looked like before, or what people had then said. Hadn't there always been a revolution?" (Phil Mailer, *Portugal: The Impossible Revolution?*)

replaced by leisurely circulation, passive consumption by active communication. Strangers strike up lively discussions on street corners. Debates continue round the clock, new arrivals constantly replacing those who depart for other activities or to try to catch a few hours of sleep, though they are usually too excited to sleep very long. While some people succumb to demagogues, others start making their own proposals and taking their own initiatives. Bystanders get drawn into the vortex, and go through astonishingly rapid changes. (A beautiful example from May 1968: The director of the national Odéon Theater was at first dismayed at its being taken over by the radical crowds; but after taking in the situation for a few minutes, he came forward and exclaimed: "Yes! Now that you have it, keep it, never give it up — burn it rather than do that!")

Of course, not everyone is immediately won over. Some people simply lay low, anticipating the time when the movement will subside and they can recover their possessions or their positions, and take their revenge. Others waver, torn between desire for change and fear of change. An opening of a few days may not be enough to break a lifetime of hierarchical conditioning. The disruption of habits and routines can be disorienting as well as liberating. Everything happens so fast it's easy to panic. Even if you manage to keep calm, it's not easy to grasp all the factors in play quickly enough to determine the best thing to do, which may appear obvious in hindsight. One of the main purposes of the present text is to point out certain typical recurring patterns so that people can be prepared to recognize and exploit such opportunities before it's too late.

Radical situations are the rare moments when qualitative change really becomes possible. Far from being abnormal, they reveal how abnormally repressed we usually are; they make our "normal" life seem like sleep-walking. Yet of the vast number of books that have been written about revolutions, few have much to say about such moments. Those dealing with the most radical modern revolts are usually merely descriptive, perhaps giving a hint of what such experiences feel like but seldom providing any useful tactical insights. Studies of bourgeois and bureaucratic revolutions are generally even less relevant. In such revolutions, where the "masses" played only a temporary supporting role for one leadership or another, their behavior could to a large degree be analyzed like the motions of physical masses, in terms of the familiar metaphors of rising and ebbing tides, pendulum swings from radicality to reaction, etc. But an antihierarchical revolution requires people to cease being homogenous, manipulable masses, to get beyond the subservience and unconsciousness that make them subject to this sort of mechanistic predictability.

Popular self-organization

During the sixties it was widely felt that the best way to foster such demassification was to form "affinity groups": small associations of close friends with compatible life-styles and perspectives. Such groups do have many obvious advantages. They can decide on a project and immediately carry it out; they are difficult to infiltrate; and when necessary they can link up with others. But even leaving aside the various pitfalls to which most of the sixties affinity groups soon succumbed, there's no getting around the fact that some matters require large-scale organization. And large groups will soon revert to accepting some sort of hierarchy unless they manage to organize themselves in a manner that renders leaders unnecessary.

One of the simplest ways for a large gathering to *begin* organizing itself is for those who have something to say to line up or sign up, with each person allowed a certain time within which they can talk about anything they want. (The Sorbonne assembly and the FSM gathering around the police car each established a three-minute limit, occasionally extended by popular acclaim.) Some of the speakers will propose specific projects that will precipitate smaller, more workable groups. ("I and some others intend to do such and such; anyone who wants to take part can join us at such and such time and place.") Others will raise issues involving the general aims or ongoing functioning of the assembly itself. (Whom does it include? When will it meet again? How will urgent new developments be dealt with in the interim? Who will be delegated to deal with specific tasks? With what degree of accountability?) In this process the participants will soon see what works and what doesn't — how strictly delegates need to be mandated, whether a chairperson is needed to facilitate discussion so that everyone isn't talking at once, etc. Many modes of organization are possible; what is essential is that things remain open, democratic and participatory, that any tendency toward hierarchy or manipulation is immediately exposed and rejected.

Despite its naïveté and confusions and lack of rigorous delegate accountability, the FSM is a good example of the spontaneous tendencies toward practical self-organization that arise in a radical situation. Some two dozen "centrals" were formed to coordinate printing, press releases, legal assistance, to rustle up food, speaker systems and other necessary supplies, or to locate volunteers who had indicated their skills and availability for different tasks. Phone trees made it possible to contact over twenty thousand students on short notice.

But beyond mere questions of practical efficiency, and even beyond the ostensible political issues, the insurgents were breaking through the whole spectacular façade and getting a taste of real life, real community. One participant estimated that within a few months he had come to know, at least as a nodding acquaintance, two or three thousand people — this at a university that was notorious for "turning people into numbers." Another movingly wrote: "Confronting an institution apparently and frustratingly designed to depersonalize and block communication, neither humane nor graceful nor responsive, we found flowering in ourselves the presence whose absence we were at heart protesting."[4]

A radical situation must spread or fail. In exceptional cases a particular location may serve as a more or less permanent base, a focus for coordination and a refuge from outside repression. (Sanrizuka, a rural region near Tokyo that was occupied by local farmers during the 1970s

---

4   One of the most powerful moments was when the sitdowners around the police car averted a potentially violent confrontation with a mob of fraternity hecklers by remaining *totally silent for half an hour*. With the wind taken out of their sails, the hecklers became bored and embarrassed, and eventually dispersed. Such collective silence has the advantage of dissolving compulsive reactions on both sides; yet because it is nonspecific it does this without the dubious content of many slogans and songs. (Singing "We Shall Overcome" has also served to calm people in difficult situations, but at the cost of sentimentalizing reality.)

The best account of the FSM is David Lance Goines's *The Free Speech Movement* (Ten Speed Press, 1993).

in an effort to block the construction of a new airport, was so stubbornly and successfully defended for so many years that it came to be used as a headquarters for diverse struggles all over Japan.) But a fixed location facilitates manipulation, surveillance and repression, and being stuck with defending it inhibits people's freedom to move around. Radical situations are always characterized by a lot of circulation: while some people converge to key locations to see what's happening, others fan out to spread the contestation to other areas.

A simple but essential step in any radical action is for people to *communicate what they are actually doing and why.* Even if what they have done is very limited, such communication is in itself exemplary: besides spreading the game to a wider field and inciting others to join in, it cuts through the usual reliance on rumors, news media and self-appointed spokespeople.

It's also a crucial step in self-clarification. A proposal to issue a collective communiqué presents concrete alternatives: Who do we want to communicate with? For what purpose? Who is interested in this project? Who agrees with this statement? Who disagrees? With which points? This may lead to a polarization as people see the different possibilities of the situation, sort out their own views, and regroup with like-minded persons to pursue diverse projects.

Such polarization clarifies matters for everyone. Each tendency remains free to express itself and to test its ideas in practice, and the results can be discerned more clearly than if contradictory strategies were mixed together in some lowest-common-denominator compromise. When people see a practical need for coordination, they will coordinate; in the mean time, the proliferation of autonomous individuals is far more fruitful than the superficial, top-down "unity" for which bureaucrats are always appealing.

Large crowds sometimes enable people to do things that would be imprudent if undertaken by isolated individuals; and certain collective actions, such as strikes or boycotts, require people to act in concert, or at least not to go against a majority decision. But many other matters can be dealt with directly by individuals or small groups. Better to strike while the iron is hot than to waste time trying to argue away the objections of masses of spectators who are still under the sway of manipulators.

The situationists in May 1968
Small groups have every right to choose their own collaborators: specific projects may require specific abilities or close accord among the participants. A radical situation opens up broader possibilities among a broader range of people. By simplifying basic issues and cutting through habitual separations, it renders masses of ordinary people capable of carrying out tasks they could not even have imagined the week before. In any case, the self-organized masses are the only ones who can carry out those tasks — no one else can do it on their behalf.

What is the role of individual radicals in such a situation? It is clear that they must not claim to represent or lead the people. On the other hand, it is absurd to declare, in the name of avoiding hierarchy, that they should immediately "dissolve into the masses" and cease putting forward their own views or initiating their own projects. They should hardly do less than the ordinary "mass" individuals, who have to express *their* views and initiate *their* projects or nothing at all would happen. In practice those radicals who claim to be afraid of "telling people what to do" or of "acting in place of the workers" generally end up either doing nothing or disguising their endless reiterations of their ideology as "reports of discussions among some workers."

The situationists and Enragés had a considerably more lucid and forthright practice during May 1968. During the first three or four days of the Sorbonne occupation (14-17 May) they openly expressed their views on the tasks of the assembly and of the general movement. On the basis of those views one of the Enragés, René Riesel, was elected to the first Sorbonne Occupation Committee, and he and his fellow delegates were reelected the following day.

Riesel and one other delegate (the rest apparently slipped away without fulfilling any of their responsibilities) endeavored to carry out the two policies he had advocated: maintaining total democracy in the Sorbonne and disseminating the most widespread appeals for occupying the factories and forming workers councils. But when the assembly repeatedly allowed its Occupation Committee to be overridden by various unelected leftist bureaucracies and failed to affirm the call for workers councils (thereby denying the workers the encouragement to do what the assembly itself was doing in the Sorbonne), the Enragés and situationists left the assembly and continued their agitation independently.

There was nothing undemocratic about this departure: the Sorbonne assembly remained free to do whatever it wanted. But when it failed to respond to the urgent tasks of the situation and even contradicted its own pretensions of democracy, the situationists felt that it had no further claim to be considered a focal point of the most radical possibilities of the movement. Their diagnosis was confirmed by the subsequent collapse of any pretense of participatory democracy at the Sorbonne: after their departure the assembly had no more elections and reverted to the typical leftist form of self-appointed bureaucrats running things over the heads of passive masses.

While this was going on among a few thousand people in the Sorbonne, millions of workers were occupying their factories throughout the country. (Hence the absurdity of characterizing May 1968 as a "student movement.") The situationists, the Enragés and a few dozen other councilist revolutionaries formed the Council for Maintaining the Occupations (CMDO) with the aim of encouraging those workers to bypass the union bureaucrats and directly link up with each other in order to realize the radical possibilities their action had already opened up.[5]

Workerism is obsolete, but workers' position remains pivotal

"Virtuous indignation is a powerful stimulant, but a dangerous diet. Keep in mind the old proverb: anger is a bad counsellor. . . . Whenever your sympathies are strongly stirred on behalf of some cruelly ill used person or persons of whom you know nothing except that

5   On May 1968 see *SI Anthology*, pp. 225-256, 343-352 [Revised Edition pp. 288-325, 435-457], and René Viénet's *Enragés and Situationists in the Occupation Movement*. Also recommended is Roger Grégoire and Fredy Perlman's *Worker-Student Action Committees, France May '68* (Black and Red, 1969).

they are ill used, your generous indignation attributes all sorts of virtues to them, and all sorts of vices to those who oppress them. But the blunt truth is that ill used people are worse than well used people."

—George Bernard Shaw, *The Intelligent Woman's Guide to Socialism and Capitalism*

"We shall abolish slaves because we can't stand the sight of them."

—Nietzsche

Fighting for liberation does not imply applauding the traits of the oppressed. The ultimate injustice of social oppression is that it is more likely to debase the victims than to ennoble them.

A lot of traditional leftist rhetoric stemmed from obsolete work-ethic notions: the bourgeois were bad because they didn't do productive work, whereas the worthy proletarians deserved the fruits of their labor, etc. As labor has become increasingly unnecessary and directed to increasingly absurd ends, this perspective has lost whatever sense it may once have had. The point is not to praise the proletariat, but to abolish it.

Class domination hasn't gone away just because a century of leftist demagogy has made some of the old radical terminology sound pretty corny. While phasing out certain kinds of traditional blue-collar labor and throwing whole sectors of the population into permanent unemployment, modern capitalism has proletarianized almost everyone else. White-collar workers, technicians, and even middle-class professionals who formerly prided themselves on their independence (doctors, scientists, scholars) are increasingly subject to the crassest commercialization and even to virtually assembly-line style regimentation.

Less than 1% of the global population owns 80% of the world's land. Even in the supposedly more egalitarian United States, economic disparity is extreme and constantly growing more extreme. Twenty years ago the average CEO salary was 35 times that of the average production worker; today it's 120 times as much. Twenty years ago the richest half-percent of the American population owned 14% of the total private wealth; they now own 30% of it. But such figures do not convey the full extent of this elite's power. The "wealth" of the lower and middle classes is almost entirely devoted to covering their day-to-day expenses, leaving little or nothing for investment at any significant, socially empowering level. A magnate who owns as little as five or ten percent of a corporation will usually be able to *control* it (due to the apathy of the unorganized mass of small stockholders), thus wielding as much power as if he owned the whole thing. And it only takes a few major corporations (whose directorates are closely interlinked with each other and with upper government bureaucracies) to buy out, wipe out or marginalize smaller independent competitors and effectively control the key politicians and media.

The omnipresent spectacle of middle-class prosperity has concealed this reality, especially in the United States where, because of its particular history (and despite the violence of many of its past class conflicts), people are more naïvely oblivious to class divisions than anywhere else in the world. The wide variety of ethnicities and the multitude of complex intermediate gradations has buffered and blurred the fundamental distinction between top and bottom. Americans own so many commodities that they fail to notice that someone else owns the whole society. Except for those at the very bottom, who can't help knowing better, they generally assume that poverty is the fault of the poor, that any enterprising person has plenty of opportunity, that if you can't make a satisfactory living in one place you can always make a fresh start somewhere else. A century ago, when people could just pick up and head further west, this belief had some foundation; the persistence of nostalgic frontier spectacles obscures the fact that present conditions are quite different and that we no longer have anywhere else to go.

The situationists sometimes used the term *proletariat* (or more precisely, *the new proletariat*) in a broadened sense, to refer to "all those who have no power over their own lives and know it." This usage may be rather loose, but it has the merit of stressing the fact that society is still divided into classes, and that the fundamental division is still between the few who own and control everything and the rest who have little or nothing to exchange but their own labor power. In some contexts it may be preferable to use other terms, such as "the people"; but not when this amounts to indiscriminately lumping exploiters with exploited.

The point is not to romanticize wage laborers, who, not surprisingly, considering that the spectacle is designed above all to keep them deluded, are often among the most ignorant and reactionary sectors of society. Nor is it a matter of scoring points to see who is most oppressed. All forms of oppression must be contested, and everyone can contribute to this contestation — women, youth, unemployed, minorities, lumpens, bohemians, peasants, middle classes, even renegades from the ruling elite. But none of these groups can achieve a definitive liberation without abolishing the material foundation of all these oppressions: the system of commodity production and wage labor. And this abolition can be achieved only through the collective *self-abolition* of wage laborers. They alone have the leverage not only to directly bring the whole system to a stop, but to start things up again in a fundamentally different way.[6]

Nor is it a matter of giving anyone special privileges. Workers in essential sectors (food, transportation, communications, etc.) who have rejected their capitalist and union bosses and begun to self-manage their own activities will obviously have no interest in holding on to the "privilege" of doing all the work and every interest in inviting everyone else, whether nonworkers or workers from obsolete sectors (law, military, sales, advertising, etc.), to join them in the project of reducing and transforming it. Everyone who takes part will share in the decisionmaking; the only ones left out will be those who remain on the sidelines claiming special privileges.

Traditional syndicalism and councilism have tended

---

6   "Labor will not only SHUT DOWN the industries, but Labor will REOPEN, under the management of the appropriate trades, such activities as are needed to preserve public health and public peace. If the strike continues, Labor may feel led to avoid public suffering by reopening more and more activities. UNDER ITS OWN MAN-AGEMENT. And that is why we say that we are starting on a road that leads — NO ONE KNOWS WHERE!" (Announcement on the eve of the 1919 Seattle general strike.) See Jeremy Brecher's *Strike!* (South End, 1972), pp. 101-114. More extensive accounts are included in *Root and Branch: The Rise of the Workers' Movements* and in Harvey O'Connor's *Revolution in Seattle*, both currently out of print.

to take the existing division of labor too much for granted, as if people's lives in a postrevolutionary society would continue to center around fixed jobs and workplaces. Even within the present society such a perspective is becoming increasingly obsolete: as most people work at absurd and frequently only temporary jobs without in any way identifying with them, while many others don't work on the wage market at all, work-related issues become merely one aspect of a more general struggle.

At the beginning of a movement it may be appropriate for workers to identify themselves as such. ("We, the workers of such and such company, have occupied our workplace with such and such aims; we urge workers in other sectors to do likewise.") The ultimate goal, however, is not the self-management of existing enterprises. For, say, media workers to have control over the media just because they happen to work there would be almost as arbitrary as the present control by whoever happens to own them. Workers' management of the particular conditions of their work will need to be combined with community management of matters of general concern. Housewives and others working in relatively separated conditions will need to develop their own forms of organization to enable them to express their own particular interests. But potential conflicts of interest between "producers" and "consumers" will be quickly superseded when everyone becomes directly involved in both aspects; when workers councils interlink with neighborhood and community councils; and when fixed work positions fade through the obsoleting of most jobs and the reorganization and rotation of those that remain (including housework and child care).

The situationists were certainly right to strive for the formation of workers councils during the May 1968 factory occupations. But it should be noted that those occupations were triggered by actions of largely nonworker youth. The post-1968 situationists tended to fall into a sort of workerism (though a resolutely anti-work-ethic one), seeing the proliferation of wildcat strikes as the major indicator of revolutionary possibilities while paying less attention to developments on other terrains. Actually, blatant union sellouts often force into wildcat struggles workers who are in other respects not particularly radical; and on the other hand, people can resist the system in many other ways besides strikes (including avoiding wage labor as much as possible in the first place). The situationists rightly recognized collective self-management and individual "radical subjectivity" as complementary and equally essential aspects of the revolutionary project, but without quite succeeding in bringing them together (though they certainly came closer than did the surrealists, who tried to link cultural and political revolt simply by declaring their fervent adhesion to one or another version of Bolshevik ideology).[7]

---

7   Raoul Vaneigem (who incidentally wrote a good brief critical history of surrealism) represented the clearest expression of both aspects. His little book *De la grève sauvage à l'autogestion généralisée* (literally "From Wildcat Strike to Generalized Self-Management," but partially translated as *Contributions to the Revolutionary Struggle*) usefully recapitulates a number of basic tactics during wildcat strikes and other radical situations as well as various possibilities of postrevolutionary social organization. Unfortunately it is also padded with the inflated verbiage characteristic of Vaneigem's post-SI writings, attributing to worker struggles a Vaneigemist content that is neither justified nor necessary. The radical-subjectivity aspect was rigidified into a tediously repeated ideology of hedonism in Vaneigem's later

Wildcats and sitdowns

Wildcat strikes do present interesting possibilities, especially if the strikers occupy their workplace. Not only does this make their position more secure (it prevents lockouts and scabbing, and the machines and products serve as hostages against repression), it brings everyone together, virtually guaranteeing collective self-management of the struggle and hinting at the idea of self-managing the whole society.

Once the usual operation has been stopped, everything takes on a different ambience. A drab workplace may be transfigured into an almost sacred space that is jealously guarded against the profane intrusion of bosses or police. An observer of the 1937 sitdown strike in Flint, Michigan, described the strikers as "children playing at a new and fascinating game. They had made a palace out of what had been their prison." (Quoted in Sidney Fine's *Sit-Down: The General Motors Strike of 1936-1937.*) Though the aim of the strike was simply to win the right to unionize, its organization was virtually councilist. During the six weeks that they lived in their factory (using car seats for beds and cars for closets) a general assembly of all 1200 workers met twice daily to determine policies regarding food, sanitation, information, education, complaints, communication, security, defense, sports and recreation, and to elect accountable and frequently rotated committees to implement them. There was even a Rumor Committee, whose purpose was to counteract disinformation by tracking down the source and checking the validity of every rumor. Outside the factory, strikers' wives took care of rounding

---

books (*The Book of Pleasures,* etc.), which read like cotton-candy parodies of the ideas he dealt with so trenchantly in his earlier works.

up food and organizing pickets, publicity, and liaison with workers in other cities. Some of the bolder ones organized a Women's Emergency Brigade which had a contingency plan to form a buffer zone in case of a police attack on the factories. "If the police want to fire then they'll just have to fire into us."

Unfortunately, although workers retain a pivotal position in some crucial areas (utilities, communication, transportation), workers in many other sectors have less leverage than they used to. Multinational companies usually have large reserves and can wait it out or shift operations to other countries, while workers have a hard time holding out without wages coming in. Far from threatening anything essential, many present-day strikes are mere appeals to postpone shutting down obsolete industries that are losing money. Thus, while the strike remains the most basic worker tactic, workers must also devise other forms of on-the-job struggle and find ways to link up with struggles on other terrains.

Consumer strikes
Like worker strikes, consumer strikes (boycotts) depend on both the leverage they can exert and the support they can enlist. There are so many boycotts in favor of so many causes that, except for a few based on some glaringly clear moral issue, most of them fail. As is so often the case in social struggles, the most fruitful consumer strikes are those in which people are fighting directly for themselves, such as the early civil rights boycotts in the South or the "self-reduction" movements in Italy and elsewhere in which whole communities have decided to pay only a certain percentage of utility bills or mass transit fares. A rent strike is a particularly simple and powerful action, but

it's difficult to achieve the degree of unity necessary to get one started except among those who have nothing to lose; which is why the most exemplary challenges to the fetish of private property are being made by homeless squatters.

In what might be called reverse boycotts, people sometimes join in *supporting* some popular institution that is threatened. Raising money for a local school or library or alternative institution is usually fairly banal, but such movements occasionally generate a salutary public debate. In 1974 striking reporters took over a major South Korean newspaper and began publishing exposés of government lies and repression. In an effort to bankrupt the paper without having to openly suppress it, the government pressured all the advertisers to remove their ads from the paper. The public responded by buying thousands of individual ads, using their space for personal statements, poems, quotations from Tom Paine, etc. The "Freedom of Speech Support Column" soon filled several pages of each issue and circulation increased significantly before the paper was finally suppressed.

But consumer struggles are limited by the fact that consumers are at the receiving end of the economic cycle: they may exert a certain amount of pressure through protests or boycotts or riots, but they don't control the mechanisms of production. In the above-mentioned Korean incident, for example, the public participation was only made possible by the workers' takeover of the paper.

A particularly interesting and exemplary form of worker struggle is what is sometimes called a "social strike" or "giveaway strike," in which people carry on with their jobs but in ways that prefigure a free social order: workers giving away goods they have produced, clerks undercharging customers, transportation workers letting everyone ride free. In February 1981 11,000 telephone workers occupied exchanges throughout British Columbia and carried on all phone services without charge for six days before being maneuvered out by their union. Besides winning many of their demands, they seem to have had a delightful time.[8] One can imagine ways of going further and becoming more selective, such as blocking business and government calls while letting personal calls go through free. Postal workers could do likewise with mail; transportation workers could continue to ship necessary goods while refusing to transport police or troops. . . .

But this type of strike would make no sense for that large majority of workers whose jobs serve no sensible purpose. (The best thing that such workers can do is to publicly denounce the absurdity of their own work, as some ad designers nicely did during May 1968.) Moreover, even useful work is often so parcelized that isolated groups of workers can implement few changes on their own. And even the small minority who happen to produce finished and salable products (as did the workers who in 1973 took over the bankrupt Lip watch factory in Besançon, France,

---

8   "One day into this thing, and I'm tired, but compared to the posi-tive sensations that are passing through this place, fatigue doesn't stand a chance. . . . Who will ever forget the look on management's faces when we tell them we are now in control, and their services are obviously no longer needed. . . . Everything as normal, except we don't collect phone bills. . . . We're also making friends from other departments. Guys from downstairs are coming up to help out and learn our jobs. . . . We're all flying. . . . Sailing on pure adrenalin. It's like we own the bloody thing. . . . The signs on the front door say, CO-OP TEL: UNDER NEW MANAGEMENT — NO MANAGEMENT ALLOWED." (Rosa Collette, "Operators Dial Direct Action," *Open Road*, Vancouver, Spring 1981.)

and started running it for themselves) usually remain dependent on commercial financing and distribution networks. In the exceptional case where such workers make a go of it on their own, they simply become one more capitalist company; more often, their self-management innovations merely end up rationalizing the operation for the benefit of the owners. A "Strasbourg of the factories" might occur if workers finding themselves in a Lip-type situation use the facilities and publicity it gives them to go farther than the Lip workers (who were struggling simply to save their jobs) by calling on others to join them in superseding the whole system of commodity production and wage labor. But this is unlikely to happen until there is a sufficiently widespread movement to enlarge people's perspectives and offset the risks — as in May 1968, when most of the factories of France were occupied:

What could have happened in May 1968

> If, in a single large factory, between 16 May and 30 May, a general assembly had constituted itself as a *council* holding all powers of decision and execution, expelling the bureaucrats, organizing its self-defense and calling on the strikers of all the enterprises to link up with it, this qualitative step could have immediately brought the movement to *the ultimate showdown*. . . . A very large number of enterprises would have followed the course thus discovered. This factory could immediately have taken the place of the dubious and in every sense eccentric

Sorbonne of the first days and have become the real center of the occupations movement: genuine *delegates* from the numerous councils that already virtually existed in some of the occupied buildings, and from all the councils that could have imposed themselves in all the branches of industry, would have rallied around this base. Such an assembly could then have proclaimed the expropriation of all capital, *including state capital;* announced that all the country's means of production were henceforth the collective property of the proletariat orga- nized in direct democracy; and appealed directly (by finally seizing some of the telecommunica- tions facilities, for example) to the workers of the entire world to support this revolution. Some people will say that such a hypothesis is utopian. We answer: It is precisely because the occupations movement was objectively at several moments *only an hour away* from such a result that it spread such terror, visible to everyone at the time in the impotence of the state and the panic of the so-called Communist Party, and since then in the conspiracy of silence concerning its gravity. [SI Anthology, pp. 234-235 [Revised Edition pp. 299-300] .]

What prevented this from happening was above all the labor unions, in particular the largest one in the country: the Communist Party-dominated CGT. Inspired by the rebellious youth who had fought the police in the streets and taken over the Sorbonne and other public buildings, ten million workers ignored their unions and occupied virtually all the factories and many of the offices in the country, launching the first wildcat general strike in history. But most of these workers were unclear enough as to what to do next that they allowed the union bureaucracy to insinuate itself into the movement it had tried to prevent. The bureaucrats did everything they could to brake and fragment the movement: calling brief token strikes; setting up phony "rank-and-file" organizations composed of loyal Party members; seizing control of the loudspeaker systems; rigging elections in favor of returning to work; and most crucially, locking the factory gates in order to keep workers isolated from each other and from the other insurgents (on the pretext of "guarding against outside provocateurs"). The unions then proceeded to negotiate with the employers and the government a package of wage and vacation bonuses. This bribe was emphatically rejected by a large majority of the workers, who had the sense, however confused, that some more radical change was on the agenda. In early June, de Gaulle's presenting the carrot/stick alternative of new elections or civil war finally intimidated many workers into returning to work. There were still numerous holdouts, but their isolation from each other enabled the unions to tell each group that all the others had resumed work, so that they would believe they were alone and give up.

Methods of confusion and cooption

As in May 1968, when the more developed countries are threatened with a radical situation, they usually rely on confusion, concessions, curfews, distractions, disinformation, fragmentation, preemption, postponement and other methods of diverting, dividing and coopting the opposition, reserving overt physical repression as a last resort.

These methods, which range from the subtle to the ludi-crous,[9] are so numerous that it would be impossible here to mention more than a few.

A common method of confusing the issues is to distort the apparent alignment of forces by projecting diverse positions onto a linear, left-versus-right schema, implying that if you are opposed to one side you must be in favor of the other. The communism-versus-capitalism spectacle served this purpose for over half a century. Since the recent collapse of that farce, the tendency has been to declare a centrist pragmatic global consensus, with any opposition being lumped with lunatic-fringe "extremisms" (fascism and religious fanaticism on the right, terrorism and "anarchy" on the left).

One of the classic divide-and-rule methods has been discussed earlier: encouraging the exploited to fragment into a multitude of narrow group identities, which can be manipulated into directing their energies into squabbling with each other. Conversely, opposed classes can be lumped together by patriotic hysteria and other means. Popular fronts, united fronts and similar coalitions serve to obscure fundamental conflicts of interest in the name of joint opposition to a common enemy (bourgeoisie + prole-tariat versus a reactionary regime; military-bureaucratic strata + peasantry versus foreign domination). In such coalitions the upper group generally has the material and ideological resources to maintain its control over the lower group, which is tricked into postponing self-organized

---

9   "A South African company is selling an anti-riot vehicle that plays disco music through a loudspeaker to soothe the nerves of would-be troublemakers. The vehicle, already bought by one black nation, which the company did not identify, also carries a water cannon and tear gas." (AP, 23 September 1979.)

action on its own behalf until it's too late. By the time victory has been attained over the common enemy, the upper group has had time to consolidate its power (often in a new alliance with elements of the defeated enemy) in order to crush the radical elements of the lower group.

Any vestige of hierarchy within a radical movement will be used to divide and undermine it. If there are no cooptable leaders, a few will be created by intensive media exposure. Leaders can be privately bargained with and held responsible for their followers; once they are coopted, they can establish similar chains of command beneath them, enabling a large mass of people to be brought under control without the rulers having to deal with all of them openly and simultaneously.

Cooption of leaders serves not only to separate them from the people, but also divides the people among themselves — some seeing the cooption as a victory, others denouncing it, others hesitating. As attention shifts from participatory actions to the spectacle of distant leader-celebrities debating distant issues, most people become bored and disillusioned. Feeling that matters are out of their hands (perhaps even secretly relieved that somebody else is taking care of them), they return to their previous passivity.

Another method of discouraging popular participation is to emphasize problems that seem to require specialized expertise. A classic instance was the ploy of certain German military leaders in 1918, at the moment when the workers and soldiers councils that emerged in the wake of the German collapse at the end of World War I potentially had the country in their hands:

On the evening of November 10, when the

Supreme Command was still at Spa, a group of seven enlisted men presented themselves at headquarters. They were the 'Executive Committee' of the Supreme Headquarters Soldiers' Council. Their demands were somewhat unclear, but obviously they expected to play a role in the command of the Army during its retreat. At the very least they wanted the right to countersign the Supreme Command's orders and to insure that the field army was not used for any counterrevolutionary purpose. The seven soldiers were courteously received by a Lieutenant Colonel Wilhelm von Faupel, who had been carefully rehearsed for the occasion. . . . Faupel led the delegates into the Supreme Command's map room. Everything was laid out on a gigantic map which occupied one wall: the huge complex of roads, railway lines, bridges, switching points, pipelines, command posts and supply dumps — the whole an intricate lace of red, green, blue and black lines converging into narrow bottlenecks at the crucial Rhine bridges. . . . Faupel then turned to them. The Supreme Command had no objection to the soldiers' councils, he said, but did his hearers feel competent to direct the general evacuation of the German Army along these lines of communication? . . . The disconcerted soldiers stared uneasily at the immense map. One of them allowed that this was not what they had really had in mind — 'This work can well be left to the officers.' In the end, the seven soldiers willingly gave the officers their support. More than this, they practically begged the officers to retain command. . . . Whenever a soldiers' council delegation appeared at Supreme Headquarters, Colonel Faupel was trotted out to repeat his earlier performance; it always worked. [Richard Watt, *The Kings Depart: Versailles and the German Revolution*.]

Terrorism reinforces the state

Terrorism has often served to break the momentum of radical situations. It stuns people, turns them back into spectators anxiously following the latest news and speculations. Far from weakening the state, terrorism seems to confirm the need to strengthen it. If terrorist spectacles fail to spontaneously arise when it needs them, the state itself may produce them by means of provocateurs. (See Sanguinetti's *On Terrorism and the State* and the last half of Debord's *Preface to the Fourth Italian Edition of "The Society of the Spectacle."*)

A popular movement can hardly prevent individuals from carrying out terrorist or other thoughtless actions, actions that may sidetrack and destroy it as surely as if they were the work of a provocateur. The only solution is to create a movement with such consistently forthright and nonmanipulative tactics that everyone will recognize individual stupidities or police provocations for what they are.

An antihierarchical revolution can only be an "open conspiracy." Obviously some things require secrecy, especially under the more repressive regimes. But even in such cases the means should not be inconsistent with the ultimate goal: the supersession of all separate power through the conscious participation of everyone. Secrecy often has the absurd result that the police are the *only* ones who know what is happening, and are thus able to infiltrate and manipulate a radical group without anyone else being aware of it. The best defense against infiltration is to make sure there's nothing of any importance to infiltrate, i.e. that no radical organization wields any separate power. The best safety is in numbers: once thousands of people are openly involved, it hardly matters if a few spies are among them.

Even in small group actions safety often lies in maximum publicity. When some of the Strasbourg scandal participants started to get cold feet and suggested toning things down, Mustapha Khayati (the SI delegate who was the main author of the *Student Poverty* pamphlet) pointed out that the safest course would not be to avoid offending the authorities too much — as if they would be grateful for being only moderately and hesitantly insulted! — but to perpetrate such a widely publicized scandal that they wouldn't dare retaliate.

The ultimate showdown

To get back to the May 1968 factory occupations, suppose that the French workers had rejected the bureaucratic maneuvers and established a councilist network throughout the country. What then?

> In such an eventuality, civil war would naturally have been inevitable. . . . Armed counterrevolution would certainly have been launched immediately. But it would not have been certain of winning. Some of the troops would obviously have mutinied; the workers would have figured out how to get weapons, and they

> certainly would not have built any more barri-
> cades — a good form of *political* expression at
> the beginning of the movement, but obviously
> ridiculous *strategically*. . . . Foreign intervention
> would have inevitably followed . . . probably
> beginning with NATO forces, but with the
> direct or indirect support of the Warsaw Pact.
> But then everything would once again have
> hinged on the European proletariat: double or
> nothing. [*SI Anthology*, p. 235 [Revised Edition
> pp. 300-301].]

Roughly speaking, the significance of armed struggle varies inversely with the degree of economic development. In the most underdeveloped countries social struggles tend to be reduced to military struggles, because without arms there is little that the impoverished masses can do that will not hurt them more than the rulers, especially when their traditional self-sufficiency has been destroyed by a one-crop economy geared for export. (But even if they win militarily, they can usually be overpowered by foreign inter-vention or pressured into compliance with the global economy, unless parallel revolutions elsewhere open up new fronts.)

In more developed countries armed force has rela-tively less significance, though it can, of course, still be an important factor at certain critical junctures. It is possible, though not very efficient, to force people to do simple manual labor at gunpoint. It is not possible to do this with people who work with paper or computers within a complex industrial society — there are too many opportu-nities for troublesome yet untraceable "mistakes." Modern capitalism requires a certain amount of cooperation and even semicreative participation from its workers. No large enterprise could function for a day without its workers' spontaneous self-organization, reacting to unforeseen problems, compensating for managers' mistakes, etc. If workers engage in a "work-to-rule" strike in which they do nothing more than strictly follow all the official regulations, the whole operation will be slowed down or even brought to a complete halt (forcing the managers, who are unable to openly condemn such strictness, into the amusingly awkward position of having to hint to the workers that they should get on with their work without being quite so rigorous). The system survives only because most workers are relatively apathetic and, in order not to cause trouble for themselves, cooperate enough to keep things going.

Isolated revolts may be repressed one at a time; but if a movement spreads fast enough, as in May 1968, a few hundred thousand soldiers and police can hardly do anything in the face of ten million striking workers. Such a movement can be destroyed only from the inside. If the people don't know what they need to do, arms can scarcely help them; if they do know, arms can scarcely stop them.

Only at certain moments are people "together" enough to revolt successfully. The more lucid rulers know that they are safe if they can only disperse such threats before they develop too much momentum and self-awareness, whether by direct physical repression or by the various sorts of diversion mentioned above. It hardly matters if the people later find out that they were tricked, that they had victory in their hands if they had only known it: once the opportunity has passed, it's too late.

Ordinary situations are full of confusions, but

matters are generally not so urgent. In a radical situation things are both simplified and speeded up: the issues become clearer, but there is less time to resolve them.

The extreme case is dramatized in a famous scene in Eisenstein's *Potemkin*. Mutinous sailors, heads covered by a tarp, have been lined up to be shot. Guards aim their rifles and are given the order to fire. One of the sailors cries out: "Brothers! Do you realize who you are shooting?" The guards waver. The order is given again. After a suspenseful hesitation the guards lower their weapons. They help the sailors to raid the armory, together they turn against the officers, and the battle is soon won.

Note that even in this violent showdown the outcome is more a matter of consciousness than of brute power: once the guards come over to the sailors, the fight is effectively over. (The remainder of Eisenstein's scene — a drawn-out struggle between an officer villain and a martyrized revolutionary hero — is mere melodrama.) In contrast to war, in which two distinct sides consciously oppose each other, "class struggle is not just a battle waged against an external enemy, the bourgeoisie; it is equally the struggle of the proletariat *against itself*: against the devastating and degrading effects of the capitalist system on its class consciousness" (Lukács, *History and Class Consciousness*). Modern revolution has the peculiar quality that the exploited majority automatically wins as soon as it becomes collectively aware of the game it is playing. The proletariat's opponent is ultimately nothing but the product of its own alienated activity, whether in the economic form of capital, the political form of party and union bureaucracies, or the psychological form of spectacular conditioning. The rulers are such a tiny minority that they would be immediately overwhelmed if they had not managed to bamboozle a large portion of the population into identifying with them, or at least into taking their system for granted; and especially into becoming divided against each other.

The tarp, which dehumanizes the mutineers, making it easier for the guards to shoot them, symbolizes this divide-and-rule tactic. The "Brothers!" shout represents the countertactic of *fraternization*.

While fraternization refutes lies about what is happening elsewhere, its greatest power probably stems from the emotional effect of direct human encounter, which reminds soldiers that the insurgents are people not essentially different from themselves. The state naturally tries to prevent such contact by bringing in troops from other regions who are unfamiliar with what has taken place and who, if possible, don't even speak the same language; and by quickly replacing them if they nevertheless become too contaminated by rebellious ideas. (Some of the Russian troops sent in to crush the 1956 Hungarian revolution were told that they were in Germany and that the people confronting them in the streets were resurgent Nazis!)

In order to expose and eliminate the most radical elements, a government sometimes deliberately provokes a situation that will lead to an excuse for violent repression. This is a dangerous game, however, because, as in the *Potemkin* incident, forcing the issue may provoke the armed forces to come over to the people. From the rulers' standpoint, the optimum strategy is to brandish just enough of a threat that there is no need to risk the ulti-mate showdown. This worked in Poland in 1980-81. The

Russian bureaucrats knew that to invade Poland might bring about their own downfall; but the constantly hinted threat of such an invasion successfully intimidated the radical Polish workers, who could easily have overthrown the state, into tolerating the persistence of military-bureaucratic forces within Poland. The latter were eventually able to repress the movement without having to call in the Russians.

Internationalism

"Those who make revolutions half way only dig their own graves." A revolutionary movement cannot attain some local victory and then expect to peacefully coexist with the system until it's ready to try for a little more. All existing powers will put aside their differences in order to destroy any truly radical popular movement before it spreads. If they can't crush it militarily, they'll strangle it economically (national economies are now so globally interdependent that no country would be immune from such pressure). The only way to defend a revolution is to *extend* it, both qualitatively and geographically. The only guarantee against internal reaction is the most radical liberation of every aspect of life. The only guarantee against external intervention is the most rapid internationalization of the struggle.

The most profound expression of internationalist solidarity is, of course, to make a parallel revolution in one's own country (1848, 1917-1920, 1968). Short of this, the most urgent task is at least to prevent counterrevolutionary intervention *from* one's own country, as when British workers pressured their government not to support the slave states during the American Civil War (even though this meant greater unemployment due to lack of cotton imports); or when Western workers struck and mutinied against their governments' attempts to support the reactionary forces during the civil war following the Russian revolution; or when people in Europe and America opposed their countries' repression of anticolonial revolts.

Unfortunately, even such minimal defensive efforts are few and far between. Positive internationalist support is even more difficult. As long as the rulers remain in control of the most powerful countries, direct personal reinforcement is complicated and limited. Arms and other supplies may be intercepted. Even communications sometimes don't get through until it's too late.

One thing that does get through is an announcement that one group is relinquishing its power or claims over another. The 1936 fascist revolt in Spain, for example, had one of its main bases in Spanish Morocco. Many of Franco's troops were Moroccan and the antifascist forces could have exploited this fact by declaring Morocco independent, thereby encouraging a revolt at Franco's rear and dividing his forces. The probable spread of such a revolt to other Arab countries would at the same time have diverted Mussolini's forces, which were supporting Franco, to defend Italy's North African possessions. But the leaders of the Spanish Popular Front government rejected this idea for fear that such an encouragement of anticolonialism would alarm France and England, from whom they were hoping for aid. Needless to say this aid never came anyway.[10]

---

10 If this question had been openly posed to the Spanish workers (who had already bypassed the vacillating Popular Front government by seizing arms and resisting the fascist coup by themselves, and in the process launched the revolution) they would probably

Similarly, if, before the Khomeiniists had been able to consolidate their power, the insurgent Iranians in 1979 had supported total autonomy for the Kurds, Baluchis and Azerbaijans, this would have won them as firm allies of the most radical Iranian tendencies and might have spread the revolution to the adjacent countries where overlapping portions of those peoples live, while simultaneously undermining the Khomeiniist reactionaries in Iran.

Encouraging others' autonomy does not imply supporting any organization or regime that might take advantage of it. It's simply a matter of leaving the Moroccans, the Kurds, or whomever to work out their own

---

have agreed to grant Moroccan independence. But once they were swayed by political leaders — including even many anarchist leaders — into tolerating that government in the name of antifascist unity, they were kept unaware of such issues.

The Spanish revolution remains the single richest revolutionary experience in history, though it was complicated and obscured by the simultaneous civil war against Franco and by the sharp contradictions within the antifascist camp — which, besides two or three million anarchists and anarchosyndicalists and a considerably smaller contingent of revolutionary Marxists (the POUM), included bourgeois republicans, ethnic autonomists, socialists and Stalinists, with the latter in particular doing everything in their power to repress the revolution. The best comprehensive histories are Pierre Broué and Emile Témime's *Revolution and the War in Spain* and Burnett Bolloten's *The Spanish Revolution* (the latter is also substantially incorporated in Bolloten's monumental final work, *The Spanish Civil War*). Some good first-hand accounts are George Orwell's *Homage to Catalonia*, Franz Borkenau's *The Spanish Cockpit*, and Mary Low and Juan Breá's *Red Spanish Notebook*. Other books worth reading include Vernon Richards's *Lessons of the Spanish Revolution*, Murray Bookchin's *To Remember Spain*, Gerald Brenan's *The Spanish Labyrinth*, Sam Dolgoff's *The Anarchist Collectives*, Abel Paz's *Durruti: The People Armed*, and Victor Alba and Stephen Schwartz's *Spanish Marxism versus Soviet Communism: A History of the P.O.U.M.*

affairs. The hope is that the example of an antihierarchical revolution in one country will inspire others to contest their own hierarchies.

It's our only hope, but not an entirely unrealistic one. The contagion of a genuinely liberated movement should never be underestimated.

Chapter 4: Rebirth

"It will, of course, be said that such a scheme as is set forth here is quite impractical, and goes against human nature. This is perfectly true. It is impractical, and it goes against human nature. This is why it is worth carrying out, and that is why one proposes it. For what is a practical scheme? A practical scheme is either a scheme that is already in existence, or a scheme that could be carried out under existing conditions. But it is exactly the existing conditions that one objects to; and any scheme that could accept these conditions is wrong and foolish. The conditions will be done away with, and human nature will change. The only thing that one really knows about human nature is that it changes. Change is the one quality we can predicate of it. The systems that fail are those that rely on the permanency of human nature, and not on its growth and development."

—Oscar Wilde, *The Soul of Man Under Socialism*

Utopians fail to envision postrevolutionary diversity
Marx considered it presumptuous to attempt to predict how people would live in a liberated society. "It will be up

to those people to decide if, when and what they want to do about it, and what means to employ. I don't feel qualified to offer them any advice on this matter. They will presumably be at least as clever as we are" (letter to Kautsky, 1 February 1881). His modesty in this regard compares favorably with those who accuse him of arrogance and authoritarianism while themselves not hesitating to project their own fancies into pronouncements as to what such a society can or cannot be.

It is true, however, that if Marx had been a little more explicit about what he envisioned, it would have been that much more difficult for Stalinist bureaucrats to pretend to be implementing his ideas. An exact blueprint of a liberated society is neither possible nor necessary, but people must have some sense of its nature and feasibility. The belief that there is no practical alternative to the present system is one of the things that keeps people resigned.

Utopian speculations can help free us from the habit of taking the status quo for granted, get us thinking about what we really want and what might be possible. What makes them "utopian" in the pejorative sense that Marx and Engels criticized is the failure to take present conditions into consideration. There is usually no serious notion of how we might get from here to there. Ignoring the system's repressive and cooptive powers, utopian authors generally envision some simplistic cumulative change, imagining that, with the spread of utopian communities or utopian ideas, more and more people will be inspired to join in and the old system will simply collapse.

I hope the present text has given some more realistic ideas of how a new society might come about. In any case, at this point I am going to jump ahead and do a little speculating myself.

To simplify matters, let us assume that a victorious revolution has spread throughout the world without too much destruction of basic infrastructures, so that we no longer need to take into consideration problems of civil war, threats of outside intervention, the confusions of disinformation or the delays of massive emergency reconstruction, and can examine some of the issues that might come up in a new, fundamentally transformed society.

Though for clarity of expression I will use the future tense rather than the conditional, the ideas presented here are simply possibilities to consider, not prescriptions or predictions. If such a revolution ever happens, a few years of popular experimentation will change so many of the variables that even the boldest predictions will soon seem laughably timid and unimaginative. All we can reasonably do is try to envision the problems we will confront at the very beginning and some of the main tendencies of further developments. But the more hypotheses we explore, the more possibilities we will be prepared for and the less likely we will be to unconsciously revert to old patterns.

Far from being too extravagant, most fictional utopias are too narrow, generally being limited to a monolithic implementation of the author's pet ideas. As Marie Louise Berneri notes in the best survey of the field (*Journey Through Utopia*), "All utopias are, of course, the expression of personal preferences, but their authors usually have the conceit to assume that their personal tastes should be enacted into laws; if they are early risers the whole of their imaginary community will have to get up at four o'clock in the morning; if they dislike women's make-up, to use it is made a crime; if they are jealous husbands infidelity will be punished by death."

If there is one thing that can be confidently predicted about the new society, it is that it will be *far more diverse* than any one person's imagination or any possible description. Different communities will reflect every sort of taste — aesthetic and scientific, mystical and rationalist, hightech and neoprimitive, solitary and communal, industrious and lazy, spartan and epicurean, traditional and experimental — continually evolving in all sorts of new and unforeseeable combinations.[1]

Decentralization and coordination

There will be a strong tendency toward decentralization and local autonomy. Small communities promote habits of cooperation, facilitate direct democracy, and make possible the richest social experimentation: if a local experiment fails, only a small group is hurt (and others can help out); if it succeeds it will be imitated and the advantage will spread. A decentralized system is also less vulnerable to accidental disruption or to sabotage. (The latter danger, however, will probably be negligible in any case: it's unlikely that a liberated society will have anywhere near the immense number of bitter enemies that are constantly produced by the present one.)

But decentralization can also foster hierarchical control by isolating people from each other. And some

---

1   P.M.'s *Bolo'bolo* (1983; new edition: Semiotext(e), 1995) has the merit of being one of the few utopias that fully recognize and welcome this diversity. Leaving aside its flippancies and idiosyncrasies and its rather unrealistic notions about how we might get there, it touches on a lot of the basic problems and possibilities of a postrevolutionary society.

things can best be organized on a large scale. One big steel factory is more energy-efficient and less damaging to the environment than a smelting furnace in every community. Capitalism has tended to overcentralize in some areas where greater diversity and self-sufficiency would make more sense, but its irrational competition has also fragmented many things that could more sensibly be standardized or centrally coordinated. As Paul Goodman notes in *People or Personnel* (which is full of interesting examples of the pros and cons of decentralization in various present-day contexts), where, how and how much to decentralize are empirical questions that will require experimentation. About all we can say is that the new society will probably decentralize as much as possible, but without making a fetish of it. Most things can be taken care of by small groups or local communities; regional and global councils will be limited to matters with broad ramifications or significant efficiencies of scale, such as environmental restoration, space exploration, dispute resolution, epidemic control, coordination of global production, distribution, transportation and communication, and maintenance of certain specialized facilities (e.g. hightech hospitals or research centers).

It is often said that direct democracy may have worked well enough in the old-fashioned town meeting, but that the size and complexity of modern societies make it impossible. How can millions of people each express their own viewpoint on every issue?

They don't need to. Most practical matters ultimately come down to a limited number of options; once these have been stated and the most significant arguments have been advanced, a decision can be reached without further ado. Observers of the 1905 soviets and the 1956 Hungarian workers councils were struck by the brevity of people's statements and the rapidity with which decisions were arrived at. Those who spoke to the point tended to get delegated; those who spouted hot air got flak for wasting people's time.

For more complicated matters, committees can be elected to look into various possibilities and report back to the assemblies about the ramifications of different options. Once a plan is adopted, smaller committees can continue to monitor developments, notifying the assemblies of any relevant new factors that might suggest modifying it. On controversial issues multiple committees reflecting opposing perspectives (e.g. protech versus antitech) might be set up to facilitate the formulation of alternative proposals and dissenting viewpoints. As always, delegates will not impose any decisions (except regarding the organization of their own work) and will be elected on a rotating and recallable basis, so as to ensure both that they do a good job and that their temporary responsibilities don't go to their heads. Their work will be open to public scrutiny and final decisions will always revert to the assemblies.

Modern computer and telecommunication technologies will make it possible for anyone to instantly check data and projections for themselves, as well as to widely communicate their own proposals. Despite current hype, such technologies do not automatically promote democratic participation; but they have the potential to facilitate it if they are appropriately modified and put under popular control.[2]

---

2 Although the so-called networking revolution has so far been limited mainly to increased circulation of spectator trivia, modern communications technologies continue to play an important role in

Telecommunications will also render delegates less necessary than during previous radical movements, when they functioned to a great extent as mere bearers of information back and forth. Diverse proposals could be circulated and discussed ahead of time, and if an issue was of sufficient interest council meetings could be hooked up live with local assemblies, enabling the latter to immediately confirm, modify or repudiate delegate decisions.

---

undermining totalitarian regimes. Years ago the Stalinist bureaucracies had to cripple their own functioning by restricting the availability of photocopy machines and even typewriters lest they be used to reproduce *samizdat* writings. The newer technologies are proving even more difficult to control:

"The conservative *Guangming Daily* reported new enforcement measures targeted at an estimated 90,000 illegal fax machines in Beijing. Chinese analysts say the regime fears that the proliferation of fax machines is allowing information to flow too freely. Such machines were used extensively during student demonstrations in 1989 that resulted in a military crackdown. . . . In the comfort of their own homes in Western capitals, such as London, oppositionists can tap out messages to activists in Saudi Arabia who, by downloading via Internet in their own homes, no longer have to fear a knock on the door in the middle of the night. . . . Every taboo subject from politics to pornography is spreading through anonymous electronic messages far beyond the government's iron grip. . . . Many Saudis find themselves discussing religion openly for the first time. Atheists and fundamentalists regularly slug it out in Saudi cyberspace, a novelty in a country where the punishment for apostasy is death. . . . But banning the Internet is not possible without removing all computers and telephone lines. . . . Experts claim that for those willing to work hard enough to get it, there is still little any government can do to totally deny access to information on the Internet. Encrypted e-mail and subscribing to out-of-country service providers are two options available to net-savvy individuals for circumventing current Internet controls. . . . If there is one thing repressive East Asian governments fear more than unrestricted access to outside media sources, it is that their nations' competitiveness in the rapidly growing information industry may be compromised. Already, protests

But when the issues are not particularly controversial, mandating will probably be fairly loose. Having arrived at some general decision (e.g. "This building should be remodeled to serve as a daycare center"), an assembly might simply call for volunteers or elect a committee to implement it without bothering with detailed account-ability.

Safeguards against abuses

Idle purists can always envision possible abuses. "Aha! Who knows what subtle elitist maneuvers these delegates and technocratic specialists may pull off!" The fact remains that large numbers of people cannot directly oversee every detail at every moment. Any society has to rely to *some* extent on people's good will and common sense. The point is that abuses are far less possible under generalized self-management than under any other form of social organization.

People who have been autonomous enough to inau-gurate a self-managed society will naturally be alert to any reemergence of hierarchy. They will note how delegates carry out their mandates, and rotate them as often as prac-ticable. For some purposes they may, like the ancient Athenians, choose delegates by lot so as to eliminate the popularity-contest and deal-making aspects of elections. In matters requiring technical expertise they will keep a wary eye on the experts until the necessary knowledge is more widely disseminated or the technology in question is

have been voiced in the business communities of Singapore, Malaysia, and China that censoring the Internet may, in the end, hamper those nations' aspirations to be the most technologically ad vanced on the block." (*Christian Science Monitor*, 11 August 1993, 24 August 1995 and 12 November 1996.)

simplified or phased out. Skeptical observers will be designated to sound the alarm at the first sign of chicanery. A specialist who provides false information will be quickly found out and publicly discredited. The slightest hint of any hierarchical plot or of any exploitive or monopolistic practice will arouse universal outrage and be eliminated by ostracism, confiscation, physical repression or whatever other means are found necessary.

These and other safeguards will always be available to those worried about potential abuses, but I doubt if they will often be necessary. On any serious issue people can insist on as much mandating or monitoring as they want to bother with. But in most cases they will probably give delegates a reasonable amount of leeway to use their own judgment and creativity.

Generalized self-management avoids both the hierarchical forms of the traditional left and the more simplistic forms of anarchism. It is not bound to any ideology, even an "antiauthoritarian" one. If a problem turns out to require some specialized expertise or some degree of "leadership," the people involved will soon find this out and take whatever steps *they* consider appropriate to deal with it, without worrying about whether present-day radical dogmatists would approve. For certain uncontroversial functions they might find it most convenient to appoint specialists for indefinite periods of time, removing them only in the unlikely event that they abuse their position. In certain emergency situations in which quick, authoritative decisions are essential (e.g. fire-fighting) they will naturally grant to designated persons whatever temporary authoritarian powers are needed.

Consensus, majority rule and unavoidable hierarchies
But such cases will be exceptional. The general rule will be
consensus when practicable, majority decision when necessary. A character in William Morris's News from
Nowhere (one of the most sensible, easygoing and down-
to-earth utopias) gives the example of whether a metal
bridge should be replaced by a stone one. At the next
Mote (community assembly) this is proposed. If there is a
clear consensus, the issue is settled and they proceed to
work out the details of implementation. But if a few of
the neighbors disagree to it, if they think that the beastly
iron bridge will serve a little longer and they don't want to
be bothered with building a new one just then, they don't
count heads that time, but put off the formal discussion to
the next Mote; and meantime arguments pro and con are
flying about, and some get printed, so that everybody
knows what is going on; and when the Mote comes
together again there is a regular discussion and at last a
vote by show of hands. If the division is a close one, the
question is again put off for further discussion; if the division is a wide one, the minority are asked if they will yield
to the more general opinion, which they often, nay, most
commonly do. If they refuse, the question is debated a
third time, when, if the minority has not perceptibly
grown, they always give way; though I believe there is
some half-forgotten rule by which they might still carry it
on further; but I say, what always happens is that they are
convinced, not perhaps that their view is the wrong one,
but they cannot persuade or force the community to adopt
it.

Note that what enormously simplifies cases like this
is that there are no longer any conflicting economic inter-

ests — no one has any means or any motive to bribe or bamboozle people into voting one way or the other because he happens to have a lot of money, or to control the media, or to own a construction company or a parcel of land near a proposed site. Without such conflicts of interest, people will naturally incline to cooperation and compromise, if only to placate opponents and make life easier for themselves. Some communities might have formal provisions to accommodate minorities (e.g. if, instead of merely voting no, 20% express a "vehement objection" to some proposal, it must pass by a 60% majority); but neither side will be likely to abuse such formal powers lest it be treated likewise when the situations are reversed. The main solution for repeated irreconcilable conflicts will lie in the wide diversity of cultures: if people who prefer metal bridges, etc., constantly find themselves outvoted by Morris-type arts-and-crafts traditionalists, they can always move to some neighboring community where more congenial tastes prevail.

Insistence on total consensus makes sense only when the number of people involved is relatively small and the issue is not urgent. Among any large number of people complete unanimity is rarely possible. It is absurd, out of worry over possible majority tyranny, to uphold a minority's right to constantly obstruct a majority; or to imagine that such problems will go away if we leave things "unstructured."

As was pointed out in a well-known article many years ago (Jo Freeman's *The Tyranny of Structurelessness*), there's no such thing as a structureless group, there are simply different types of structures. An unstructured group generally ends up being dominated by a clique that does have some effective structure. The unorganized members have no means of controlling such an elite, especially when their antiauthoritarian ideology prevents them from admitting that it exists.

Failing to acknowledge majority rule as a backup when unanimity is not attainable, anarchists and consensists are often unable to arrive at practical decisions except by following those de facto leaders who are skilled at maneuvering people into unanimity (if only by their capacity to endure interminable meetings until all the opposition has got bored and gone home). Fastidiously rejecting workers councils or anything else with any taint of coercion, they themselves usually end up settling for far less radical lowest-common-denominator projects.

It's easy to point out shortcomings in the workers councils of the past, which were, after all, just hurried improvisations by people involved in desperate struggles. But if those brief efforts were not perfect models to blindly imitate, they nevertheless represent the most practical step in the right direction that anyone has come up with so far. *Riesel's article on councils* (*SI Anthology,* pp. 270-282 [Revised Edition pp. 348-362]) discusses the limitations of these old movements, and rightly stresses that council power should be understood as the sovereignty of the popular assemblies as a whole, not merely of the councils of delegates they have elected. Some groups of radical workers in Spain, wishing to avoid any ambiguity on this latter point, have referred to themselves as "assemblyists" rather than "councilists." One of the CMDO leaflets (*SI Anthology,* p. 351 [Revised Edition p. 444]) specifies the following essential features of councilist democracy:

- Dissolution of all external power
- Direct and total democracy
- Practical unification of decision and execution
- Delegates who can be revoked at any moment by those who have mandated them
- Abolition of hierarchy and independent specializations
- Conscious management and transformation of all the conditions of liberated life
- Permanent creative mass participation
- Internationalist extension and coordination

Once these features are recognized and implemented, it will make little difference whether people refer to the new form of social organization as "anarchy," "communalism," "communist anarchism," "council communism," "libertarian communism," "libertarian socialism," "participatory democracy" or "generalized self-management," or whether its various overlapping components are termed "workers councils," "antiwork councils," "revolutionary councils," "revolutionary assemblies," "popular assemblies," "popular committees," "communes," "collectives," "kibbutzes," "bolos," "motes," "affinity groups," or anything else. ("Generalized self-management" is unfortunately not very catchy, but it has the advantage of referring to both means and goal while being free of the misleading connotations of terms like "anarchy" or "communism.")

In any case, it's important to remember that large-scale formal organization will be the exception. Most local matters can be handled directly and informally. Individuals or small groups will simply go ahead and do what seems appropriate in any given situation ("adhocracy"). Majority rule will merely be a *last resort* in the progressively diminishing number of cases in which conflicts of interest cannot otherwise be resolved.

A nonhierarchical society does not mean that everyone magically becomes equally talented or must participate equally in everything; it simply means that *materially based and reinforced* hierarchies have been eliminated. Although differences of abilities will undoubtedly diminish when everyone is encouraged to develop their fullest potentials, the point is that whatever differences remain will no longer be transformed into differences of wealth or power.

People will be able to take part in a far wider range of activities than they do now, but they won't have to rotate all positions all the time if they don't feel like it. If someone has a special taste and knack for a certain task, others will probably be happy to let her do it as much as she wants — at least until someone else wants a shot at it. "Independent specializations" (monopolistic control over socially vital information or technologies) will be abolished; open, nondominating specializations will flourish. People will still ask more knowledgeable persons for advice when they feel the need for it (though if they are curious or suspicious they will always be encouraged to investigate for themselves). They will still be free to voluntarily submit themselves as students to a teacher, apprentices to a master, players to a coach or performers to a director — remaining equally free to discontinue the relation at any time. In some activities, such as group folksinging, anyone can join right in; others, such as performing a classical concerto, may require rigorous training and coherent direction, with some people taking leading roles, others following, and others being happy just to listen. There should be plenty of opportunity for both types. The situationist critique of the spectacle is a critique of an excessive tendency in present society; it does not imply that everyone must be an "active participant" twenty-four hours a day.

Apart from the care necessary for mental incompetents, the only unavoidable enforced hierarchy will be the temporary one involved in raising children until they are capable of managing their own affairs. But in a safer and saner world children could be given considerably more freedom and autonomy than they are now. When it comes to openness to the new playful possibilities of life, adults may learn as much from them as vice versa. Here as elsewhere, the general rule will be to let people find their own level: a ten-year-old who takes part in some project might have as much say in it as her adult co-participants, while a nonparticipating adult will have none.

Self-management does not require that everyone be geniuses, merely that most people not be total morons. It's the *present* system that makes unrealistic demands — pretending that the people it systematically imbecilizes are capable of judging between the programs of rival politicians or the advertising claims of rival commodities, or of engaging in such complex and consequential activities as raising a child or driving a car on a busy freeway. With the supersession of all the political and economic pseudoissues that are now intentionally kept incomprehensible, most matters will turn out not to be all that complicated.

When people first get a chance to run their own lives

they will undoubtedly make lots of mistakes; but they will soon discover and correct them because, unlike hierarchs, they will have no interest in covering them up. Self-management does not guarantee that people will always make the right decisions; but any other form of social organization guarantees that someone else will make the decisions for them.

Eliminating the roots of war and crime

The abolition of capitalism will eliminate the conflicts of interest that now serve as a pretext for the state. Most present-day wars are ultimately based on economic conflicts; even ostensibly ethnic, religious or ideological antagonisms usually derive much of their real motivation from economic competition, or from psychological frustrations that are ultimately linked to political and economic repression. As long as desperate competition prevails, people can easily be manipulated into reverting to their traditional groupings and squabbling over cultural differences they wouldn't bother about under more comfortable circumstances. War involves far more work, hardship and risk than any form of constructive activity; people with real opportunities for fulfillment will have more interesting things to do.

The same is true for crime. Leaving aside victimless "crimes," the vast majority of crimes are directly or indirectly related to money and will become meaningless with the elimination of the commodity system. Communities will then be free to experiment with various methods for dealing with whatever occasional antisocial acts might still occur.

There are all sorts of possibilities. The persons involved might argue their cases before the local community or a "jury" chosen by lot, which would strive for the most reconciling and rehabilitating solutions. A convicted offender might be "condemned" to some sort of public service — not to intentionally unpleasant and demeaning shitwork administered by petty sadists, which simply produces more anger and resentment, but to meaningful and potentially engaging projects that might introduce him to healthier interests (ecological restoration, for example). A few incorrigible psychotics might have to be humanely restrained in one way or another, but such cases would become increasingly rare. (The present proliferation of "gratuitous" violence is a predictable reaction to social alienation, a way for those who are not treated as real persons to at least get the grim satisfaction of being recognized as real threats.) Ostracism will be a simple and effective deterrent: the thug who laughs at the threat of harsh punishment, which only confirms his macho prestige, will be far more deterred if he knows that everyone will give him the cold shoulder. In the rare case where that proves inadequate, the variety of cultures might make banishment a workable solution: a violent character who was constantly disturbing a quiet community might fit in fine in some more rough-and-tumble, Wild West-type region — or face less gentle retaliation.

Those are just a few of the possibilities. Liberated people will undoubtedly come up with more creative, effective and humane solutions than any we can presently imagine. I don't claim that there will be no problems, only that there will be far fewer problems than there are now, when people who happen to find themselves at the bottom of an absurd social order are harshly punished for their crude efforts to escape, while those at the top loot the planet with impunity.

The barbarity of the present penal system is surpassed only by its stupidity. Draconian punishments have repeatedly been shown to have no significant effect on the crime rate, which is directly linked to levels of poverty and unemployment as well as to less quantifiable but equally obvious factors like racism, the destruction of urban communities, and the general alienation produced by the commodity-spectacle system. The threat of years in prison, which might be a powerful deterrent to someone with a satisfying life, means little to those with no meaningful alternatives. It is hardly very brilliant to slash already pitifully inadequate social programs in the name of economizing, while filling prisons with lifers at a cost of close to a million dollars each; but like so many other irrational social policies, this trend persists because it is reinforced by powerful vested interests.[3]

---

3   "In the post-Cold War era politicians have discovered crime-baiting as a substitute for red-baiting. Just as the fear of communism propelled the unimpeded expansion of the military-industrial complex, crime-baiting has produced the explosive growth of the correctional-industrial complex, also known as the crime-control industry. Those who disagree with its agenda of more prisons are branded criminal sympathizers and victim betrayers. Since no politician will risk the 'soft on crime' label, an unending spiral of destructive policies is sweeping the country. ... Repression and brutalization will be further promoted by the institutions that are the primary beneficiaries of such policies. As California increased its prison population from 19,000 to 124,000 over the past 16 years, 19 new prisons were built. With the increase in prisons, the California Correctional Peace Officers Association (CCPOA), the guards' union, emerged as the state's most powerful lobby. ... As the percentage of the state budget devoted to higher education has fallen from 14.4 percent to 9.8 percent, the share of the budget for corrections has risen from 3.9 percent to 9.8 percent. The average salary and bene-

Abolishing money

A liberated society must abolish the whole money-commodity economy. To continue to accept the validity of money would amount to accepting the continued dominance of those who had previously accumulated it, or who had the savvy to reaccumulate it after any radical reapportionment. Alternative forms of "economic" reckoning will still be needed for certain purposes, but their carefully limited scope will tend to diminish as increasing material abundance and social cooperativity render them less necessary.

A postrevolutionary society might have a three-tier economic setup along the following lines:

1. Certain basic goods and services will be freely available to everyone without any accounting whatsoever.
2. Others will also be free, but only in limited, rationed quantities.
3. Others, classified as "luxuries," will be available in exchange for "credits."

Unlike money, credits will be applicable only to certain specified goods, not to basic communal property such as land, utilities or means of production. They will also prob-

---

fits for prison guards in California exceeds $55,000 — the highest in the nation. This year the CCPOA, along with the National Rifle Association, has directed its substantial war chest to promote the passage of the 'three strikes, you're out' initiative that would triple the current size of California's prison system. The same dynamics that evolved in California will certainly result from Clinton's crime bill. As more resources are poured into the crime-control industry, its power and influence will grow." (Dan Macallair, *Christian Science Monitor*, 20 September 1994.)

ably have expiration dates to limit any excessive accumulation.

Such a setup will be quite flexible. During the initial transition period the amount of free goods might be fairly minimal — just enough to enable a person to get by — with most goods requiring earning credits through work. As time goes on, less and less work will be necessary and more and more goods will become freely available — the tradeoff between the two factors always remaining up to the councils to determine. Some credits might be generally distributed, each person periodically receiving a certain amount; others might be bonuses for certain types of dangerous or unpleasant work where there is a shortage of volunteers. Councils might set fixed prices for certain luxuries, while letting others follow supply and demand; as a luxury becomes more abundant it will become cheaper, perhaps eventually free. Goods could be shifted from one tier to another depending on material conditions and community preferences.

Those are just some of the possibilities.[4] Experi-

---

4   Other possibilities are presented in considerable detail in *Workers' Councils and the Economics of a Self-Managed Society* (London Solidarity's edition of a *Socialisme ou Barbarie* article by Cornelius Castoriadis). This text is full of valuable suggestions, but I feel that it assumes more centering around work and workplace than will be necessary. Such an orientation is already somewhat obsolete and will probably become much more so after a revolution.

Michael Albert and Robin Hahnel's *Looking Forward: Participatory Economics for the Twenty First Century* (South End, 1991) also includes a number of useful points on self-managed organization. But the authors assume a society in which there is still a money economy and the workweek is only slightly reduced (to around 30 hours). Their hypothetical examples are largely modeled on present-day worker co-ops and the "economic participation" envisaged includes voting on marketing issues that will be superseded in a noncapitalist

menting with different methods, people will soon find out for themselves what forms of ownership, exchange and reckoning are necessary.

In any case, whatever "economic" problems may remain will not be serious because scarcity-imposed limits will be a factor only in the sector of inessential "luxuries." Free universal access to food, clothing, housing, utilities, health care, transportation, communication, education and cultural facilities could be achieved almost immediately in the industrialized regions and within a fairly short period in the less developed ones. Many of these things already exist and merely need to be made more equitably available; those that don't can easily be produced once social energy is diverted from irrational enterprises.

Take housing, for example. Peace activists have frequently pointed out that everyone in the world could be decently housed at less than the cost of a few weeks of global military expenditure. They are no doubt envisioning a fairly minimal sort of dwelling; but if the amount of energy people now waste earning the money to enrich landlords and real estate speculators was diverted to building new dwellings, everyone in the world could soon be housed very decently indeed.

To begin with, most people might continue living where they are now and concentrate on making dwellings available for homeless people. Hotels and office buildings could be taken over. Certain outrageously extravagant estates might be requisitioned and turned into dwellings, parks, communal gardens, etc. Seeing this trend, those

society. As we will see, such a society will also have a far shorter workweek, reducing the need to bother with the complicated schemes for equal rotation among different types of jobs that oc-cupy a large part of the book.

possessing relatively spacious properties might offer to temporarily quarter homeless people while helping them build homes of their own, if only to deflect potential resentment from themselves.

The next stage will be raising and equalizing the quality of dwellings. Here as in other areas, the aim will probably not be a rigidly uniform equality ("everyone must have a dwelling of such and such specifications"), but people's general sense of fairness, with problems being dealt with on a flexible, case-by-case basis. If someone feels he is getting the short end of the stick he can appeal to the general community, which, if the grievance is not completely absurd, will probably bend over backward to redress it. Compromises will have to be worked out regarding who gets to live in exceptionally desirable areas for how long. (They might be shared around by lot, or leased for limited periods to the highest bidders in credit auctions, etc.) Such problems may not be solved to everyone's complete satisfaction, but they will certainly be dealt with much more fairly than under a system in which accumulation of magic pieces of paper enables one person to claim "ownership" of a hundred buildings while others have to live on the street.

Once basic survival needs are taken care of, the quantitative perspective of labor time will be transformed into a qualitatively new perspective of free creativity. A few friends may work happily building their own home even if it takes them a year to accomplish what a professional crew could do more efficiently in a month. Much more fun and imagination and love will go into such projects, and the resulting dwellings will be far more charming, variegated and personal than what today passes for "decent." A nineteenth-century rural French mailman named Ferdinand Cheval spent all his spare time for several decades constructing his own personal fantasy castle. People like Cheval are considered eccentrics, but the only thing unusual about them is that they continue to exercise the innate creativity we all have but are usually induced to repress after early childhood. A liberated society will have lots of this playful sort of "work": personally chosen projects that will be so intensely engaging that people will no more think of keeping track of their "labor time" than they would of counting caresses during lovemaking or trying to economize on the length of a dance.

Absurdity of most present-day labor

Fifty years ago Paul Goodman estimated that less than ten percent of the work then being done would satisfy our basic needs. Whatever the exact figure (it would be even lower now, though it would of course depend on precisely what we consider basic or reasonable needs), it is clear that most present-day labor is absurd and unnecessary. With the abolition of the commodity system, hundreds of millions of people now occupied with producing superfluous commodities, or with advertising them, packaging them, transporting them, selling them, protecting them or profiting from them (salespersons, clerks, foremen, managers, bankers, stockbrokers, landlords, labor leaders, politicians, police, lawyers, judges, jailers, guards, soldiers, economists, ad designers, arms manufacturers, customs inspectors, tax collectors, insurance agents, investment advisers, along with their numerous underlings) will all be freed up to share the relatively few actually necessary tasks.

Add the unemployed, who according to a recent UN report now constitute over 30% of the global population.

If this figure seems large it is because it presumably includes prisoners, refugees, and many others who are not usually counted in official unemployment statistics because they have given up trying to look for work, such as those who are incapacitated by alcoholism or drugs, or who are so nauseated by the available job options that they put all their energy into evading work through crimes and scams.

Add millions of old people who would love to engage in worthwhile activities but who are now relegated to a boring, passive retirement. And teenagers and even younger children, who would be excitedly challenged by many useful and educational projects if they weren't confined to worthless schools designed to instill ignorant obedience.

Then consider the large component of waste even in undeniably necessary work. Doctors and nurses, for example, spend a large portion of their time (in addition to filling out insurance forms, billing patients, etc.) trying with limited success to counteract all sorts of socially induced problems such as occupational injuries, auto accidents, psychological ailments and diseases caused by stress, pollution, malnutrition or unsanitary living conditions, to say nothing of wars and the epidemics that often accompany them — problems that will largely disappear in a liberated society, leaving health-care providers free to concentrate on basic preventive medicine.

Then consider the equally large amount of *intentionally* wasted labor: make-work designed to keep people occupied; suppression of labor-saving methods that might put one out of a job; working as slowly as one can get away with; sabotaging machinery to exert pressure on bosses, or out of simple rage and frustration. And don't forget all the absurdities of "Parkinson's Law" (work expands to fill the time available), the "Peter Principle" (people rise to their level of incompetence) and similar tendencies that have been so hilariously satirized by C. Northcote Parkinson and Laurence Peter.

Then consider how much wasted labor will be eliminated once products are made to last instead of being designed to fall apart or go out of style so that people have to keep buying new ones. (After a brief initial period of high production to provide everyone with durable, high-quality goods, many industries could be reduced to very modest levels — just enough to keep those goods in repair, or to occasionally upgrade them whenever some truly significant improvement is developed.)

Taking all these factors into consideration, it's easy to see that in a sanely organized society the amount of necessary labor could be reduced to one or two days per week.

Transforming work into play

But such a drastic quantitative reduction will produce a qualitative change. As Tom Sawyer discovered, when people are not forced to work, even the most banal task may become novel and intriguing: the problem is no longer how to get people to do it, but how to accommodate all the volunteers. It would be unrealistic to expect people to work full time at unpleasant and largely meaningless jobs without surveillance and economic incentives; but the situation becomes completely different if it's a matter of putting in ten or fifteen hours a week on worthwhile, varied, self-organized tasks of one's choice.

Moreover, many people, once they are engaged in projects that interest them, will not want to limit themselves to the minimum. This will reduce necessary tasks to an even more minuscule level for others who may not have such enthusiasms.

There's no need to quibble about the term *work*. Wage work needs to be abolished; meaningful, freely chosen work can be as much fun as any other kind of play. Our present work usually produces practical results, but not the ones we would have chosen, whereas our free time is mostly confined to trivialities. With the abolition of wage labor, work will become more playful and play more active and creative. When people are no longer driven crazy by their work, they will no longer require mindless, passive amusements to recover from it.

Not that there's anything wrong with enjoying trivial pastimes; it's simply a matter of recognizing that much of their present appeal stems from the absence of more fulfilling activities. Someone whose life lacks real adventure may derive at least a little vicarious exoticism from collecting artifacts from other times and places; someone whose work is abstract and fragmented may go to great lengths to actually produce a whole concrete object, even if that object is no more significant than a model ship in a bottle. These and countless other hobbies reveal the persistence of creative impulses that will really blossom when given free play on a broader scale. Imagine how people who enjoy fixing up their home or cultivating their garden will get into recreating their whole community; or how the thousands of railroad enthusiasts will jump at the chance to rebuild and operate improved versions of the rail networks that will be one of the main ways to reduce automobile traffic.

When people are subjected to suspicion and oppressive regulations, they naturally try to get away with doing as little as possible. In situations of freedom and mutual trust there is a contrary tendency to take pride in doing the best job possible. Although some tasks in the new society will be more popular than others, the few really difficult or unpleasant ones will probably get more than enough volunteers, responding to the thrill of the challenge or the desire for appreciation, if not out of a sense of responsibility. Even now many people are happy to volunteer for worthy projects if they have the time; far more will do so once they no longer have to constantly worry about providing for the basic needs of themselves and their families. At worst, the few totally unpopular tasks will have to be divided up into the briefest practicable shifts and rotated by lot until they can be automated. Or there might be auctions to see if anyone is willing to do them for, say, five hours a week in lieu of the usual workload of ten or fifteen; or for a few extra credits.

Uncooperative characters will probably be so rare that the rest of the population may just let them be, rather than bothering to pressure them into doing their small share. At a certain degree of abundance it becomes simpler not to worry about a few possible abuses than to enlist an army of timekeepers, accountants, inspectors, informers, spies, guards, police, etc., to snoop around checking every detail and punishing every infraction. It's unrealistic to expect people to be generous and cooperative when there isn't much to go around; but a large material surplus will create a large "margin of abuse," so that it won't matter if some people do a little less than their share, or take a little more.

The abolition of money will prevent anyone from taking *much* more than their share. Most misgivings about the feasibility of a liberated society rest on the ingrained assumption that money (and thus also its necessary protector: the state) would still exist. This money-state partnership creates unlimited possibilities for abuses (legis-lators bribed to sneak loopholes into tax laws, etc.); but once it is abolished both the motives and the means for such abuses will vanish. The abstractness of market rela-tions enables one person to anonymously accumulate wealth by indirectly depriving thousands of others of basic necessities; but with the elimination of money any signifi-cant monopolization of goods would be too unwieldy and too visible.

Whatever other forms of exchange there may be in the new society, the simplest and probably most common form will be gift-giving. The general abundance will make it easy to be generous. Giving is fun and satisfying, and it eliminates the bother of accounting. The only calculation is that connected with healthy mutual emulation. "The neighboring community donated such and such to a less well off region; surely we can do the same." "They put on a great party; let's see if we can do an even better one." A little friendly rivalry (who can create the most delicious new recipe, cultivate a superior vegetable, solve a social problem, invent a new game) will benefit everyone, even the losers.

A liberated society will probably function much like a potluck party. Most people enjoy preparing a dish that will be enjoyed by others; but even if a few people don't bring anything there's still plenty to go around. It's not essential that everyone contribute an exactly equal share, because the tasks are so minimal and are spread around so widely that no one is overburdened. Since everyone is openly involved, there's no need for checking up on people or instituting penalties for noncompliance. The only element of "coercion" is the approval or disapproval of the other participants: appreciation provides positive reinforcement, while even the most inconsiderate person realizes that if he consistently fails to contribute he will start getting funny looks and might not be invited again. Organization is necessary only if some problem turns up. (If there are usually too many desserts and not enough main dishes, the group might decide to coordinate who will bring what. If a few generous souls end up bearing an unfair share of the cleanup work, a gentle prodding suffices to embarrass others into volunteering, or else some sort of systematic rotation is worked out.)

Now, of course, such spontaneous cooperation is the exception, found primarily where traditional communal ties have persisted, or among small, self-selected groups of like-minded people in regions where conditions are not too destitute. Out in the dog-eat-dog world people naturally look out for themselves and are suspicious of others. Unless the spectacle happens to stir them with some senti-mental human-interest story, they usually have little concern for those outside their immediate circle. Filled with frustrations and resentments, they may even take a malicious pleasure in spoiling other people's enjoyments.

But despite everything that discourages their humanity, most people, if given a chance, still like to feel that they are doing worthy things, and they like to be appreciated for doing them. Note how eagerly they seize the slightest opportunity to create a moment of mutual recognition, even if only by opening a door for someone or exchanging a few banal remarks. If a flood or earthquake or some other emergency arises, even the most selfish and cynical person often plunges right in, working twenty-four hours a day to rescue people, deliver food and first-aid supplies, etc., without any compensation but others' gratitude. This is why people often look back on wars and natural disasters with what might seem like a surprising degree of nostalgia. Like revolution, such events break through the usual social separations, provide everyone with opportunities to do things that really matter, and produce a strong sense of community (even if only by uniting people against a common enemy). In a liberated society these sociable impulses will be able to flourish without requiring such extreme pretexts.

Technophobic objections
Present-day automation often does little more than throw some people out of work while intensifying the regimentation of those who remain; if any time is actually gained by "labor-saving" devices, it is usually spent in an equally alienated passive consumption. But in a liberated world computers and other modern technologies could be used to eliminate dangerous or boring tasks, freeing everyone to concentrate on more interesting activities.

Disregarding such possibilities, and understandably disgusted by the current misuse of many technologies, some people have come to see "technology" itself as the main problem and advocate a return to a simpler lifestyle. How much simpler is debated — as flaws are discovered in each period, the dividing line keeps getting pushed farther back. Some, considering the Industrial Revolution as the main villain, disseminate computer-printed eulogies of hand craftsmanship. Others, seeing the invention of agriculture as the original sin, feel we should return to a hunter-gatherer society, though they are not entirely clear about what they have in mind for the present human population which could not be sustained by such an economy. Others, not to be outdone, present eloquent arguments proving that the development of language and rational thought was the real origin of our problems. Yet others contend that the whole human race is so incorrigibly evil that it should altruistically extinguish itself in order to save the rest of the global ecosystem.

These fantasies contain so many obvious self-contradictions that it is hardly necessary to criticize them in any detail. They have questionable relevance to actual past societies and virtually no relevance to present possibilities. Even supposing that life was better in one or another previous era, *we have to begin from where we are now.* Modern technology is so interwoven with all aspects of our life that it could not be abruptly discontinued without causing a global chaos that would wipe out billions of people. Postrevolutionary people will probably decide to reduce human population and phase out certain industries, but this can't be done overnight. We need to seriously consider how we will deal with all the practical problems that will be posed in the interim.

If it ever comes down to such a practical matter, I doubt if the technophobes will really want to eliminate motorized wheelchairs; or pull the plug on ingenious computer setups like the one that enables physicist Stephen Hawking to communicate despite being totally paralyzed; or allow a woman to die in childbirth who could be saved by technical procedures; or accept the reemergence of diseases that used to routinely kill or permanently disable a large percentage of the population; or resign themselves to never visiting or communicating with people in other parts of the world unless they're within walking distance; or stand by while people die in famines that could be averted through global food shipments.

The problem is that meanwhile this increasingly fashionable ideology deflects attention from real problems and possibilities. A simplistic Manichean dualism (nature is Good, technology is Bad) enables people to ignore complex historical and dialectical processes; it's so much easier to blame everything on some primordial evil, some sort of devil or original sin. What begins as a valid questioning of excessive faith in science and technology ends up as a desperate and even less justified faith in the return of a primeval paradise, accompanied by a failure to engage the present system in any but an abstract, apocalyptical way.[5]

Technophiles and technophobes are united in treating technology in isolation from other social factors, differing only in their equally simplistic conclusions that new technologies are automatically empowering or automatically alienating. As long as capitalism alienates all human

---

5   Fredy Perlman, author of one of the most sweeping expressions of this tendency, *Against His-story, Against Leviathan!* (Black and Red, 1983), provided his own best critique in his earlier book about C. Wright Mills, *The Incoherence of the Intellectual* (Black and Red, 1970): "Yet even though Mills rejects the passivity with which men accept their own fragmentation, he no longer struggles against it. The coherent self-determined man becomes an exotic creature who lived in a distant past and in extremely different material circumstances. . . . The main drift is no longer the program of the right which can be opposed by the program of the left; it is now an external spectacle which follows its course like a disease. . . . The rift between theory and practice, thought and action, widens; political ideals can no longer be translated into practical projects."

productions into autonomous ends that escape the control of their creators, technologies will share in that alienation and will be used to reinforce it. But when people free themselves from this domination, they will have no trouble rejecting those technologies that are harmful while adapting others to beneficial uses.

Certain technologies — nuclear power is the most obvious example — are indeed so insanely dangerous that they will no doubt be brought to a prompt halt. Many other industries which produce absurd, obsolete or superfluous commodities will, of course, cease automatically with the disappearance of their commercial rationales. But many technologies (electricity, metallurgy, refrigeration, plumbing, printing, recording, photography, telecommunications, tools, textiles, sewing machines, agricultural equipment, surgical instruments, anesthetics, antibiotics, among dozens of other examples that will come to mind), however they may presently be misused, have few if any *inherent* drawbacks. It's simply a matter of using them more sensibly, bringing them under popular control, introducing a few ecological improvements, and redesigning them for human rather than capitalistic ends.

Other technologies are more problematic. They will still be needed to some extent, but their harmful and irrational aspects will be phased out, usually by attrition. If one considers the automobile industry as a whole, including its vast infrastructure (factories, streets, highways, gas stations, oil wells) and all its inconveniences and hidden costs (traffic jams, parking, repairs, insurance, accidents, pollution, urban destruction), it is clear that any number of alternative methods would be preferable. The fact remains that this infrastructure is already there. The new society will thus undoubtedly continue to use existing automobiles and trucks for a few years, while concentrating on developing more sensible modes of transportation to gradually replace them as they wear out. Personal vehicles with nonpolluting engines might continue indefinitely in rural areas, but most present-day urban traffic (with a few exceptions such as delivery trucks, fire engines, ambulances, and taxis for disabled people) could be superseded by various forms of public transit, enabling many freeways and streets to be converted to parks, gardens, plazas and bike paths. Airplanes will be retained for intercontinental travel (rationed if necessary) and for certain kinds of urgent shipments, but the elimination of wage labor will leave people with time for more leisurely modes of travel — boats, trains, biking, hiking.

Here, as in other areas, it will be up to the people involved to experiment with different possibilities to see what works best. Once people are able to determine the aims and conditions of their own work, they will naturally come up with all sorts of ideas that will make that work briefer, safer and more pleasant; and such ideas, no longer patented or jealously guarded as "business secrets," will rapidly spread and inspire further improvements. With the elimination of commercial motives, people will also be able to give appropriate weight to social and environmental factors along with purely quantitative labor-time considerations. If, say, production of computers currently involves some sweatshop labor or causes some pollution (though far less than classic "smokestack" industries), there's no reason to believe that better methods cannot be figured out once people set their minds to it — very likely precisely through a judicious use of computer automation.

(Fortunately, the more repetitive the job, the easier it usually is to automate.)

The general rule will be to simplify basic manufactures in ways that facilitate optimum flexibility. Techniques will be made more uniform and understandable, so that people with a minimal general training will be able to carry out construction, repairs, alterations and other operations that formerly required specialized training. Basic tools, appliances, raw materials, machine parts and architectural modules will probably be standardized and mass-produced, leaving tailor-made refinements to small-scale "cottage industries" and the final and potentially most creative aspects to the individual users. Once time is no longer money we may, as William Morris hoped, see a revival of elaborate "labor"-intensive arts and crafts: joyful making and giving by people who care about their creations and the people for whom they are destined.

Some communities might choose to retain a fair amount of (ecologically sanitized) heavy technology; others might opt for simpler lifestyles, though backed up by technical means to facilitate that simplicity or for emergencies. Solar-powered generators and satellite-linked telecommunications, for example, would enable people to live off in the woods with no need for power and telephone lines. If earth-based solar power and other renewable energy sources proved insufficient, immense solar receptors in orbit could beam down a virtually unlimited amount of pollution-free energy.

Most Third World regions, incidentally, lie in the sun belt where solar power can be most effective. Though their poverty will present some initial difficulties, their traditions of cooperative self-sufficiency plus the fact that they are not encumbered with obsolete industrial infrastructures may give them some compensating advantages when it comes to creating new, ecologically appropriate structures. By drawing *selectively* on the developed regions for whatever information and technologies they themselves decide they need, they will be able to skip the horrible "classic" stage of industrialization and capital accumulation and proceed directly to postcapitalist forms of social organization. Nor will the influence necessarily be all one way: some of the most advanced social experimentation in history was carried out during the Spanish revolution by illiterate peasants living under virtually Third World conditions.

Nor will people in developed regions need to accept a drab transitional period of "lowered expectations" in order to enable less developed regions to catch up. This common misconception stems from the false assumption that most present-day products are desirable and necessary — implying that more for others means less for ourselves. In reality, a revolution in the developed countries will immediately supersede so many absurd commodities and concerns that even if supplies of certain goods and services are temporarily reduced, people will still be better off than they are now even in material terms (in addition to being far better off in "spiritual" terms). Once their own immediate problems are taken care of, many of them will enthusiastically assist less fortunate people. But this assistance will be voluntary, and most of it will not entail any serious self-sacrifice. To donate labor or building materials or architectural know-how so that others can build homes for themselves, for example, will not require dismantling one's own home. The potential richness of modern society consists not only of material goods, but of knowledge, ideas, techniques, inventiveness, enthusiasm, compassion, and other qualities that are actually *increased* by being shared around.

Ecological issues

A self-managed society will naturally implement most present-day ecological demands. Some are essential for the very survival of humanity; but for both aesthetic and ethical reasons, liberated people will undoubtedly choose to go well beyond this minimum and foster a rich biodiversity.

The point is that we can debate such issues open-mindedly only when we have eliminated the profit incentives and economic insecurity that now undermine even the most minimal efforts to defend the environment (loggers afraid of losing their jobs, chronic poverty tempting Third World countries to cash in on their rain forests, etc.).[6]

When humanity as a species is blamed for environmental destruction, the specific social causes are forgotten. The few who make the decisions are lumped with the powerless majority. Famines are seen as nature's revenge against overpopulation, natural checks that must be allowed to run their course — as if there was anything natural about the World Bank and the International Monetary Fund, which force Third World countries to cultivate

---

6   Isaac Asimov and Frederick Pohl's *Our Angry Earth: A Ticking Ecological Bomb* (Tor, 1991) is among the more cogent summaries of this desperate situation. After demonstrating how inadequate current policies are for dealing with it, the authors propose some drastic reforms that might postpone the worst catastrophes; but such reforms are unlikely to be implemented as long as the world is dominated by the conflicting interests of nation-states and multinational corporations.

products for export rather than food for local consumption. People are made to feel guilty for using cars, ignoring the fact that auto companies (by buying up and sabotaging electric transit systems, lobbying for highway construction and against railroad subsidies, etc.) have created a situation in which most people have to have cars. Spectacular publicity gravely urges everyone to reduce energy consumption (while constantly inciting everyone to consume more of everything), though we could by now have developed more than enough clean and renewable energy sources if the fossil-fuel companies had not successfully lobbied against devoting any significant research funding to that end.

The point is not to blame even the heads of those companies — they too are caught in a grow-or-die system that impels them to make such decisions — but to abolish the setup that continually produces such irresistible pressures.

A liberated world should have room both for human communities and for large enough regions of undisturbed wilderness to satisfy most of the deep ecologists. Between those two extremes I like to think that there will be all sorts of imaginative, yet careful and respectful, human interactions *with* nature. Cooperating with it, working with it, playing with it; creating variegated interminglings of forests, farms, parks, gardens, orchards, creeks, villages, towns.

Large cities will be broken up, spaced out, "greened," and rearranged in a variety of ways incorporating and surpassing the visions of the most imaginative architects and city planners of the past (who were usually limited by their assumption of the permanence of capitalism).

Exceptionally, certain major cities, especially those of some aesthetic or historical interest, will retain or even amplify their cosmopolitan features, providing grand centers where diverse cultures and lifestyles can come together.[7]

Some people, drawing on the situationists' early "psychogeographical" explorations and "unitary urbanism" ideas, will construct elaborate changeable decors designed to facilitate labyrinthine wanderings among diverse ambiences — Ivan Chtcheglov envisioned "assemblages of castles, grottos, lakes," "rooms more conducive to dreams than any drug," and people living in their own personal "cathedrals" (*SI Anthology*, pp. 3-4 [Revised Edition p. 6]). Others may incline more to the Far Eastern poet's definition of happiness as living in a hut beside a mountain stream.

If there aren't enough cathedrals or mountain streams to go around, maybe some compromises will have to be worked out. But if places like Chartres or Yosemite are presently overrun, this is only because the rest of the planet has been so uglified. As other natural areas are revitalized and as human habitats are made more beautiful and interesting, it will no longer be necessary for a few exceptional sites to accommodate millions of people desperate to get away from it all. On the contrary, many people may actually gravitate toward the most miserable regions because these will be the "new frontiers" where the most

---

7   For a wealth of suggestive insights on the advantages and draw-backs of different types of urban communities, past, present and potential, I recommend two books: Paul and Percival Goodman's *Communitas* and Lewis Mumford's *The City in History*. The latter is one of the most penetrating and comprehensive surveys of human society ever written.

exciting transformations will be taking place (ugly buildings being demolished to make way for experimental reconstruction from scratch).

The blossoming of free communities

The liberation of popular creativity will generate lively communities surpassing Athens, Florence, Paris and other famous centers of the past, in which full participation was limited to privileged minorities. While some people may choose to be relatively solitary and self-sufficient (hermits and nomads will be free to keep to themselves except for a few minimal arrangements with nearby communities), most will probably prefer the pleasure and convenience of doing things together, and will set up all sorts of public workshops, libraries, laboratories, laundries, kitchens, bakeries, cafés, health clinics, studios, music rooms, auditoriums, saunas, gyms, playgrounds, fairs, flea markets (without forgetting some quiet spaces to counterbalance all the socializing). City blocks might be converted into more unified complexes, connecting outer buildings with hallways and arcades and removing fences between back yards so as to create larger interior park, garden or nursery areas. People could choose among various types and degrees of participation, e.g. whether to sign up for a couple days per month of cooking, dishwashing or gardening entitling them to eat at a communal cafeteria, or to grow most of their own food and cook for themselves.

In all these hypothetical examples it's important to bear in mind the diversity of cultures that will develop. In one, cooking might be seen as a tedious chore to be minimized as much as possible and precisely apportioned; in another it might be a passion or a valued social ritual that will attract more than enough enthusiastic volunteers.

Some communities, like Paradigm III in *Communitas* (allowing for the fact that the Goodmans' schema still assumes the existence of money), may maintain a sharp distinction between the free sector and the luxury sector. Others may develop more organically integrated social patterns, along the lines of Paradigm II of the same book, striving for maximum unity of production and consumption, manual and intellectual activity, aesthetic and scientific education, social and psychological harmony, even at the cost of purely quantitative efficiency. The Paradigm III style might be most appropriate as a initial transitional form, when people are not yet used to the new perspectives and want some fixed economic frame of reference to give them a sense of security against potential abuses. As people get the bugs out of the new system and develop more mutual trust, they will probably tend more toward the Paradigm II style.

As in Fourier's charming fantasies, but minus his eccentricities and with much more flexibility, people will be able to engage in a variety of pursuits according to elaborately interrelated affinities. A person might be a regular member of certain ongoing groupings (affinity group, council, collective, neighborhood, town, region) while only temporarily taking part in various ad hoc activities (as people do today in clubs, hobbyist networks, mutual-aid associations, political-issue groups and barnraising-type projects). Local assemblies will keep tallies of offers and requests; make known the decisions of other assemblies and the current state of projects in progress or problems yet unresolved; and form libraries, switchboards and computer networks to gather and disseminate information of all kinds and to link up people with common tastes.

Media will be accessible to everyone, enabling them to express their own particular projects, problems, proposals, critiques, enthusiasms, desires, visions. Traditional arts and crafts will continue, but merely as one facet of continuously creative lives. People will still take part, with more zest than ever, in sports and games, fairs and festivals, music and dancing, lovemaking and child raising, building and remodeling, teaching and learning, camping and traveling; but new genres and arts of life will also develop that we can now hardly imagine.

More than enough people will gravitate to socially necessary projects, in agronomy, medicine, engineering, educational innovation, environmental restoration and so on, for no other reason than that they find them interesting and satisfying. Others may prefer less utilitarian pursuits. Some will live fairly quiet domestic lives; others will go in for daring adventures, or live it up in feasts and orgies; yet others may devote themselves to bird-watching, or exchanging zines, or collecting quaint memorabilia from prerevolutionary times, or any of a million other pursuits. Everyone can follow their own inclinations. If some sink into a passive spectator existence, they'll probably eventually get bored and try more creative ventures. Even if they don't, that will be their affair; it won't harm anyone else.

For anyone who finds the earthly utopia too insipid and really wants to get away from it all, the exploration and colonization of the solar system — perhaps eventually even migration to other stars — will provide a frontier that will never be exhausted.

But so will explorations of "inner space."

More interesting problems
An antihierarchical revolution will not solve all our prob-

lems; it will simply eliminate some of the anachronistic ones, freeing us to tackle *more interesting problems.*

If the present text seems to neglect the "spiritual" aspects of life, this is because I wanted to stress some basic material matters that are often overlooked. But these material matters are only the framework. A liberated society will be based far more on joy and love and spontaneous generosity than on rigid rules or egoistic calculations. We can probably get a more vivid sense of what it might be like from visionaries like Blake or Whitman than from pedantic debates about economic credits and recallable delegates.

I suspect that once people's basic material needs are generously taken care of and they are no longer subjected to a constant barrage of commercial titillation, most of them (after brief binges of overindulgence in things they were previously deprived of) will find the greatest satisfaction in relatively simple and uncluttered lifestyles. The erotic and gustatory arts will undoubtedly be enriched in many ways, but simply as facets of full, rounded lives that also include a wide range of intellectual, aesthetic and spiritual pursuits.

Education, no longer limited to conditioning young people for a narrow role in an irrational economy, will become an enthusiastic lifelong activity. In addition to whatever formal educational institutions there may still be, people will have instant access via books and computers to information on any subject they wish to explore, and they'll be able to get hands-on experience in all sorts of arts and skills, or to seek out anyone for personal instruction or discussion — like the ancient Greek philosophers debating in the public marketplace, or the medieval

Chinese monks wandering the mountains in search of the most inspiring Zen master.

The aspects of religion that now serve as mere psychological escapes from social alienation will fade away, but the basic questions that have found more or less distorted expression in religion will remain. There will still be pains and losses, tragedies and frustrations, people will still face sickness, old age and death. And in the process of trying to figure out what, if anything, it all means, and how to deal with it, some of them will rediscover what Aldous Huxley, in *The Perennial Philosophy*, refers to as the "highest common factor" of human consciousness.

Others may cultivate exquisite aesthetic sensibilities like the characters in Murasaki's *Tale of Genji*, or develop elaborate metacultural genres like the "glass bead games" in Hermann Hesse's novel (freed from the material limits that formerly confined such pursuits to narrow elites).

I like to think that as these diverse pursuits are alternated, combined and developed, there will be a general tendency toward the personal reintegration envisioned by Blake, and toward the genuine "I-Thou" relations envisioned by Martin Buber. A permanent spiritual revolution in which joyous communion does not preclude rich diversity and "generous contention." *Leaves of Grass*, Whitman's wishful thinking about the potentialities of the America of his day, perhaps comes as close as anything to conveying the expansive state of mind of such communities of fulfilled men and women, ecstatically working and playing, loving and loitering, strolling down the never-ending Open Road.

With the proliferation of continually developing and mutating cultures, travel could once again become an unpredictable adventure. The traveler could "see the cities and learn the ways of many different peoples" without the dangers and disappointments faced by the wanderers and explorers of the past. Drifting from scene to scene, from encounter to encounter; but occasionally stopping, like those barely visible human figures in Chinese landscape paintings, just to gaze into the immensity, realizing that all our doings and sayings are just ripples on the surface of a vast, unfathomable universe.

These are just a few hints. We aren't limited to radical sources of inspiration. All sorts of creative spirits of the past have manifested or envisioned some of our almost unlimited possibilities. We can draw on any of them as long as we take care to extricate the relevant aspects from their original alienated context.

The greatest works do not so much tell us something new as remind us of things we have forgotten. We all have intimations of what life can be like at its richest — memories from early childhood, when experiences were still fresh and unrepressed, but also occasional later moments of love or camaraderie or enthusiastic creativity, times when we can't wait to get up in the morning to continue some project, or simply to see what the new day will bring. Extrapolating from these moments probably gives the best idea of what the whole world could be like. A world, as Whitman envisions it,

> Where the men and women think lightly of the laws,
> Where the slave ceases, and the master of slaves
> ceases,
> Where the populace rise at once against the never-
> ending audacity of elected persons, . . .
> Where children are taught to be laws to themselves,

and to depend on themselves,
Where equanimity is illustrated in affairs,
Where speculations on the soul are encouraged,
Where women walk in public processions in the
    streets the same as the men,
Where they enter the public assembly and take places
    the same as the men . . . .
The main shapes arise!
Shapes of Democracy total, result of centuries,
Shapes ever projecting other shapes,
Shapes of turbulent manly cities,
Shapes of the friends and home-givers of the whole
    earth,
Shapes bracing the earth and braced with the whole
    earth.

Lightning Source UK Ltd.
Milton Keynes UK
UKOW05f2006170217
294712UK00006B/44/P